M000286542

Networking in the 21ˢᵗ Century
On Linkedin:
Creating Online Relationships
And Opportunities

3rd Edition

SAM -
YOU KNOW THIS STUFF
ALREADY. BUT I
WANTED TO ADD TO
YOUR BOOK COLLECTION!

DAVID J.P. FISHER

A RockStar Publishing Book

Copyright ©2015 - 2021 David J.P. Fisher
All Rights Reserved

Edited by David Aretha

All rights reserved. Published in the United States by RockStar Publishing, Evanston, Illinois. No part of this book may be reproduced, scanned, or distributed in any printed or electronic form without written permission from the publisher. Please do not participate in or encourage piracy of copyrighted material in violation of the author's rights.

Cover Design: Debbie O'Byrne & JetLaunch

Print (Hardcover) ISBN: 978-1-944730-18-5
Print (Softcover) ISBN: 978-1-944730-16-1
E-Book ISBN: 978-1-944730-17-8

For Chrissie, Colette, and Amy
Still my cheering section over all these years

Contents

Section 3 —Craft a RockStar LinkedIn Profile

Section 4 —Find and Engage Your Network

Section 5 —Share Your Message

Foreword

My friend David J.P. Fisher, who we all call D. Fish, is an expert in three things. He gets networking, he gets sales, and he gets social media. When you put those things together, it's no surprise that he's written an incredibly practical guide to using LinkedIn.

D. Fish knows networking. In college, he developed his chops at Cutco Cutlery, selling knives face-to-face to consumers in their kitchens. That's a great way to learn how to build and strengthen professional relationships quickly. Through this experience, D. Fish learned early on that creating a strong and trusted network is foundational to sales success.

And he certainly knows sales, which is all about getting buy in. He's run his own business for over 15 years. And in 2021, Badger Mapping recognized his career as a sales professional and industry thought leader by inducting him into the company's Sales Hall of Fame.

Most importantly for the topic of this book, he gets social media. Or rather, he understands how to use social media to create meaningful connections and make things happen. And I'm talking about more than just LinkedIn. I once watched him entertain his bored toddler – who is obsessed with fighter jets – by showing him Blue Angels and Thunderbirds aerobatics via YouTube videos so he could continue in a meeting. That's how you deploy social media in a pinch!

Given all of his experience and expertise, it's no surprise that David has written an eminently useful and readable book about how professionals can network on LinkedIn, build their personal brand, and leverage new platform features. I've been part of the LinkedIn family for more than seven years and through my work editing the LinkedIn Sales blog, authoring our annual State of Sales report and more, I've become familiar with the opportunities for salespeople and LinkedIn members at large. I know firsthand that in **Networking in the 21st Century on LinkedIn,** D. Fish has created a resource that answers the questions on how to use LinkedIn more effectively.

In these pages, you'll find advice that you can immediately put into action to maximize LinkedIn as a tool to drive your career and achieve your professional goals. D. Fish provides sharp insights into how to build your personal brand, connect with the important contacts you'd like to meet, and engage with the network that you build on LinkedIn.

You'll find powerful insights into the approaches that will help build a strong presence on LinkedIn. But this isn't a boring, cookie-cutter approach. As D. Fish told me in an interview once: "You can't look at a platform with over 700 million users and say there's only one way to use it."

And that's the key to this book no matter your goals: Use it! There is a great blueprint waiting for you in the coming pages. Turn the page and take the first step to upping your LinkedIn game.

—Sean Callahan, Senior Manager of
Content Marketing at LinkedIn

PS: One more thing about D. Fish. He's passionate about good writing – so much so, that he even writes poetry. In fact, a few years ago he published **Five Seven Five**, a book of enchanting haikus about

Chicago. So, in closing, I leave you with a haiku I wrote to celebrate this book:

This book on LinkedIn
Will help you use the platform
D. Fish gets it right

Introduction

When I first wrote *Networking in the 21st Century on LinkedIn* back in 2014, I knew that the clock was ticking. Even at the point, the platform changed rapidly, and it was obvious that any book would only capture a moment in time and then be out of date quickly. So the need for a second edition and now this third edition wasn't a surprise. But what has surprised me is how much has needed updating. I thought that I would only need minor tweaks here and there. Instead, both times I overhauled over a quarter of the book! Because not only does LinkedIn keep changing, but how we use it keeps changing as well. And to understand how to use LinkedIn effectively, you have to know more than the evolving features and functions. You also have to know how it fits into the larger context of our business interactions and relationships.

Over the past two decades, LinkedIn has secured its place as the pre-eminent professional social media platform. While other sites like Twitter, Instagram, or Facebook might be sexier, LinkedIn remains the place where professionals come to share what's happening and connect with their peers, clients, partners, employees, and prospects. The LinkedIn profile has become our online "professional record of note" and is a trusted information source about the people we interact with in our daily business lives. Checking in on the newsfeed, posting a piece of content, polishing our profile, and researching others has become a regular part of many professionals' routines. You need to know the best practices to use the different parts of the platform to share your professional brand clearly and to communicate with your network.

How we use it has evolved as LinkedIn has matured and integrated itself into our business life. Over the past few years, it has grown to over 700 million members around the world, added and refined countless features like Sales Navigator and native video, and gotten itself bought by Microsoft. But what has really driven the need for updates is how LinkedIn's place in our day-to-day business has changed. The new functionalities enable us to use LinkedIn differently, and more importantly, the offline context around LinkedIn keeps changing. When I first wrote **Networking in the 21st Century on LinkedIn**, many professionals still didn't use LinkedIn regularly. That had started to shift before 2020, but the COVID-19 pandemic and the social distancing it brought accelerated the adoption of LinkedIn by a broader segment of the business world. When we couldn't connect and network in person, we had to find a replacement. And LinkedIn was already there to provide that online venue to connect and engage.

Over the past few editions, I've had to change a lot of material to stay abreast of the updates. But what hasn't changed is the overall mission of the book: help people build their professional relationships and their network using LinkedIn. My original intent was to provide a guide for how to use LinkedIn to move business forward. And that remains the same. In today's hyper-connected business world your network is a key tool to find success. How you engage with others, or how you fail to engage with others, has a profound impact on your available opportunities. Whether you are a salesperson, business owner, entrepreneur, executive, or anyone else, your ability to create connections is a huge asset that can help you achieve your professional goals. LinkedIn provides a powerful tool to help you do just that and has done so for a while.

> *What hasn't changed is the overall mission of the book: help people build their professional relationships and their network using LinkedIn.*

I started training and coaching people on LinkedIn in 2007 as part of my consulting firm, RockStar Consulting. In the early days, I wasn't so much training as I was evangelizing. I remember having to tell people, "It's LinkedIn.com. No, it's not Linked.In or Linked.com." I was also the Director of Training for Ajax Workforce Marketing, the first company to be an official partner with LinkedIn for training and branding in North America. We supported companies like Dell, Microsoft, and Fidelity as they took the first steps into social selling and online employee advocacy. In my time I have trained and coached thousands of professionals from fields as diverse as financial services, sales, marketing, software engineering, and accounting (to name just a few). I've worked with everyone from recent college grads just entering their first job to executives at some of the largest companies in the world.

In this edition of *Networking in the 21ˢᵗ Century on LinkedIn*, you'll find a host of tactical steps to craft your online brand, build your network, and share content with your connections. But just as importantly, you'll find the strategic map to think about how your LinkedIn activity fits into your business life. Your offline and online networks are an important part of your career growth and it's critical that you integrate the two in a work environment that we're creating after the arrival of COVID-19. Trying to build your career without using LinkedIn is still possible, but it's a lot harder. It's one of the tools that successful professionals are leveraging now and that they will continue to lean on for the foreseeable future. But it doesn't help to have the tools if you don't have a plan. In these pages, I want to provide the blueprints that allow you to use the tool that is LinkedIn to catapult you to online and offline success.

> *In these pages, I want to provide the blueprints that allow you to use the tool that is LinkedIn to catapult you to online and offline success.*

To that end we're going to examine the strategies and tactics that will help you take LinkedIn from just another thing on your to-do list to a key tool in engaging with your network. Our focus is on using it to improve your business relationships, both the ones you already have and the ones you are hoping to start. No matter your professional goals right now, who you know is an important part of your career success! And even more importantly, *who knows you, and who knows what you can do,* is a key piece of the process. LinkedIn is a great medium to make sure that you are connecting with a broad collection of networking partners and reinforcing your message when you engage with them.

That's why this book isn't meant to be a completely comprehensive overview of LinkedIn. The social media world moves super-fast and is in a constant state of evolution. If I dove into the minutiae of LinkedIn, it would be out-of-date before the book got to print. That's why I'm not going to look at every single button and feature on LinkedIn. Because in the end, this isn't a book about the LinkedIn website itself. This is a book on defining yourself as a professional, connecting with others, and sharing your message. LinkedIn is simply the medium to do that.

It's also important to understand that there isn't one "right" way to approach LinkedIn. You've probably noticed that there are a lot of LinkedIn books out there, and a lot of opinions on how to use it. A platform this big, with a wide variety of users, isn't going to be a one-size-fits-all affair. There are many ways to approach social media and LinkedIn. You can approach it from a marketing perspective to become a "thought leader" and develop a following. You can take a social selling approach that uses it to develop a strong customer pipeline and find useful business intelligence. You can use it as a job search tool to find the next opportunity. You can look at it as a collaboration tool that allows for easy dialogue with people around the country and globe. And so many other ways.

All of those are valuable approaches, and I would suggest that relationships are the foundation for all of them. We're going to approach LinkedIn as a social networking tool, and that network can help you no matter what your professional goals. Whether you are building a business, finding new clients, or looking for a new employer or employee, your reputation, credibility, and visibility are a key to making business happen. And that's how we want to use LinkedIn: as a tool to build those relationships and facilitate engagement in our professional lives.

Ultimately, this book isn't just about LinkedIn. It's about getting things done by using LinkedIn. It is about the results you can create from your online activity that will position you to achieve your professional goals. I want to give you the guide to moving your career forward online – so that you create the offline success that you are striving for.

> *This book isn't just about LinkedIn. It's about getting things done by using LinkedIn.*

See you on LinkedIn!

David J. P. Fisher
Evanston, Illinois
May 2021

How to Use This Book

This book is a strategic and tactical roadmap to guide your LinkedIn activity. But it's not designed to be a step-by-step manual on how to navigate LinkedIn. The site is in a constant state of flux so if I tried to do that it would be out-of-date before it made it off the printing press (or onto your Kindle). Features, capabilities, and the user interface are always changing.

Many of the chapters are hands-on and do explain different functions. But with all adjustments and new features, it's easy to get lost. If there's a question that the book can't answer, I recommend doing a quick Google search: "LinkedIn _____." That way you will get the most up-to-date information. I won't be offended if you look on someone else's site!

Each of the chapters in this book stands on its own. In fact, many started their lives as articles and blog posts on various sites. That means you can dip in and refer to sections in any order and you will be just fine. Think of it as a cookbook that has the recipes for your social media success. Where you should start will depend a lot on what you are trying to "cook." It's OK if you don't read it straight through. Feel free to skip around to the parts that are most relevant to you right now.

But there is a "method to the madness," and each section of the book builds upon the previous ones. You will be rewarded when you start at the beginning and read straight through. This is especially useful if you want to create a cohesive LinkedIn strategy. If you have been cobbling together an approach to LinkedIn, now is the perfect time to go step-by-step and create a strategic process.

We start with Section 1, where we will explore how to fit your online activity within the broader context of your professional life. To maximize your effectiveness, it's crucial that your LinkedIn activities align with your larger business goals. From there we explore your online personal brand in Section 2. We will walk through the questions you need to answer to create a clear and targeted personal brand. And that naturally moves us into Section 3. That's where we look at the tactical steps that will allow you to communicate your brand through your LinkedIn profile.

If you stop right there, you'll be ahead of most professionals. But there are a lot of activities that pay big dividends on LinkedIn. Once you have a clear online presence, the next step is to grow your network. Connecting with other professionals and sharing information with them is one of the main uses of LinkedIn. In Section 4 we'll look at how to find, connect, and engage with other professionals on LinkedIn. And in Section 5, you'll learn the tools and tricks necessary to share content effectively with your network.

These five sections will give you the full range of tools necessary to engage productively and meaningfully on LinkedIn. But there's no "perfect" way to use LinkedIn and there's no "perfect" way to use this book. The key is to make it perfect for you!

Online Resources

This is a relatively rare book on social media because you won't find any pictures in it. There's a reason that it's not full of screenshots with arrows and circles that walk you through each feature and functionality. LinkedIn is well known for consistent and regular updates to their user interface. It's also common for LinkedIn to roll out features in stages, which makes it very possible for two users to have a different experience at the exact same time. Any screenshots I included would be outdated and irrelevant within weeks.

But fear not! I've got you covered. Visit the website for this book where you can find up-to-date screenshots that highlight specific functionalities. Just click on the chapter that you are looking for. In fact, I suggest having it open in a browser on your device:

www.davidjpfisher.com/linkedinnetworking

Even if you don't have access to the screenshots, each chapter will make sense. We're not going to focus on what buttons to push, but on how to reinforce and leverage your online relationships in a way that moves business forward.

Section 1

CLARIFY YOUR SOCIAL NETWORKING STRATEGY

L inkedIn, Instagram, Facebook. Oh my!

It's easy to get overwhelmed with all the digital tools that are available. There are just so many options. To be successful, you need to approach your LinkedIn activity with a clear strategy. It's important to look at your online presence within the context of your broader business goals. This is the critical step that will take LinkedIn from a timewaster to a key part of your daily business life. In this section, we are going to look at the strategic questions and answers that should precede your tactical activities when using digital communication.

Digital is the New Normal

L et me set the stage. It's the fall of 1960. And for the first time in American history, two presidential candidates, Richard Nixon and John F. Kennedy, are going to debate each other publicly on an invention that is only a generation old: television. It's the first time that a presidential debate has been televised. Both are capable candidates and experienced politicians, but that's not what the electorate would see in that debate, and it became a deciding factor in the election.

Kennedy is widely regarded as having "won" the first debate. Presenting himself as poised and confident, he had the aura of a movie star. He had spent the previous days with his campaign team planning for the debate and rehearsing his responses. Nixon had just finished a grueling campaign tour and had recently been in the hospital. He came off as tired, pale, and disheveled. He didn't want any makeup, so when he started to sweat under the lights, he looked sweaty and just, well, bad.

Kennedy and his team had understood the power of the new medium. The opportunity for the charismatic politician to communicate with so many people at once wasn't to be underestimated. And they put the time into getting it right. While it wasn't the only factor in Kennedy's win, the debates influenced many of the American voters. Considering the outcome was determined by less the 125,000 popular votes, it's easy to see that a different outcome in the debate could have swung things in Nixon's favor.

You might not be running for President of the United States, but my guess is that you have goals that you are trying to accomplish in your career. As a professional you are trying to communicate with your colleagues, your clients, and your potential clients. Whether you like it or not, social media is the new media. It's the way that we communicate with each other, and it's not going away. According to Domo.com's annual "Data Never Sleeps" study, in 2020 Facebook users uploaded 147,000 photos, YouTube users uploaded 500 hours of video, and Instagram users uploaded 347,222 stories…every minute. Engaging with others online is here to stay.

Whether you like it or not, social media is the new media.

Yet I still talk to many professionals who don't think they have a social media problem because they can't see it. They don't see the prospects and partners going elsewhere after visiting a poorly built LinkedIn profile. They pay lip service to building their social media competence and presence, but rarely take action because they are "too busy," "company rules won't let me," or "their network isn't online." They are happy to keep doing things the way they've always done them. There's only one problem: They are going to wake up one morning in the very near future and they will have become irrelevant.

You have two paths to choose from. You can be proactive and make sure that you communicate effectively with your network online. Or you can refuse to acknowledge the shifts in how we communicate and hope for the best.

Which side of history do you want to be on?

1.2

LinkedIn Is a Tool, Not a Magic Pill

As you go through your workday today, you will focus on solving as many problems as you can. For most of us, that is what our work consists of: solving challenges that pop up through the day. Luckily our society has advanced a bit so the problems that we face aren't the dire ones that our ancestors faced, like mystery blights destroying our crops or hordes of marauding barbarians. For us, it might be finding prospective clients, balancing the books, or managing different personalities on a project.

Just like our ancestors, we consistently look to technology to solve our problems. They used irrigation and walls. We use social media and high-speed internet connections. However, if we think all we need to do is add technology, we'll wind up disappointed. Technology is a very useful tool, but it's *just a tool*. For example, it's not the hammer alone that helps construct the building. It's the hammer in the hands of someone who knows how to use it that can build a house, a hospital, or a library.

Technology is a very useful tool, but it's just a tool.

LinkedIn and other social media sites are fantastic for professional networking and connecting. Used correctly, these sites are incredibly useful and help build stronger networks and individual relationships, which leads to more and better business. But anyone who is bad at networking and relationship-building and tries to put the Band-Aid of LinkedIn over the problem just becomes someone who is bad at networking with less time on their hands.

Don't look to technology to be the shortcut solution to business problems. That new website, iPad app, or payment service might be a part of the solution, but it can only be a *part* of the solution. If you don't put in the effort to solve your challenges at a foundational level, they'll just pop up again down the line. For example, if your organization is incredibly chaotic, just giving everyone a new time-management program will only be a short-term fix. In the same way, if you don't have enough clients and think a LinkedIn profile will solve all your problems you are going to be disappointed. You need to focus on the roots of a problem (which is rarely easy and rarely quick). You need to develop the skills and abilities that will determine how well you use the technology, just like the craftsman must learn how to use a hammer well.

There are no easy answers to the challenges we face. The empty promise of social media is that it is the only answer you need. Don't be fooled. Yes, you're reading a book on improving your LinkedIn presence, but fit these strategies and tactics into your general relationship and communication skills. By integrating the online tools with your offline goals, you'll find more success. And that means that you do have to invest in your offline skills as well. Then the social media tools at your disposal will amplify your efforts to build better relationships.

1.3

Multi-Channel Communication

There has been an ever-growing number of communication tools available to us over the last century, and even more in the past few decades. It used to be that the only way to talk to someone was to find them and actually *speak* to them (or maybe mail them a letter). Now with the rush of new technologies, there's a virtual buffet of options when you want to reach out to someone.

It's important to remember, though, that not all forms of communication are created equally. This is especially true in the business world, and even more critical when having a conversation where your goal is to influence someone else's actions (for example, a sales meeting). Business success is often based on relationships, and relationships are based on communicating. Don't get trapped in using a communication method because it's convenient. It might not be that *effective*.

Think of the various communication tools that are available. What are the scenarios where they are appropriate and effective? Where are they a bad fit?

- Face-to-Face Conversation
- Video Conferencing/Webinar
- Video (Zoom) Call
- Telephone Conversation
- Written Note/Letter
- Voicemail
- Email
- Text Messaging
- Social Media Direct Messages
- LinkedIn Post
- Facebook Wall Post
- Tweet

It's pretty obvious that there's a wide spectrum of efficiency and effectiveness in this list. Your ability to choose which medium to use is almost as important as the message you want to share. How do you choose which channel to use? Human communication is complex and nuanced, so there isn't a one-size-fits-every-situation answer. But there are general rules of thumb to follow. For example, it is better when we can see the person we're speaking to. A great deal of interpersonal communication is in our body language and facial expressions. That's why face-to-face communication or video platforms are useful. But if that's not possible, it's still more effective to hear the tone of their voice than to not. Texting or emailing is easier and can be done in environments where you wouldn't be able to hear or talk, but they don't have as much depth.

Does it mean that every time you want to effectively communicate with someone you need to speak to them face-to-face? Of course not. But it does mean that you need to be strategic with how you choose to interact. Tools like LinkedIn add a lot of options to the mix, but it's important to ensure that they fit with the conversation you are trying to have. If you need to ask somebody for an important introduction, a LinkedIn InMail might not be the best choice. Do you have a quick update on a project that you would like everyone to know about? Then the status update feature is perfect. By using the proper tools and technologies, you'll find it's much easier to communicate and influence others.

We all know someone who hides behind online communication. Don't be that person.

1.4

Make Online Networking Human-to-Human

t's easy to be overwhelmed by social media. It seems like there's a new platform popping up every day, the established sites are constantly adding features, and the experts keep sharing new ways to use it. There are always new widgets, new buttons, and new functions. It would be tempting (and easier) to write off social media as a fad or just throw up your hands in surrender. But it's an immensely powerful business tool. You probably don't need every website *de jour*, but underneath the sometimes-confusing veneer are new and exciting ways for you to connect with people. Instead of getting stuck in the features and buttons, take a cue from one of the basic sales lessons I learned when I was new to the business world.

I got my professional start selling cutlery in people's kitchens (and there isn't anything as old school as direct in-home sales). One of the best pieces of advice I received in the beginning was the sales adage: "People do business with those they know, like, and trust. So to be successful, the people you want to work with have to know, like, and trust you."

People do business with those they know, like, and trust.

Here's my suggestion: let this be your guiding principle with social media. Don't freeze when you think of what steps to take online; simply ask yourself this question, "If my success in networking depends on helping people know, like, and trust me, what functionality on LinkedIn will help me accomplish that?"

This gives you a foundation that allows you to create an effective online strategy – on LinkedIn and beyond. It will be a strategy that is uniquely suited to your needs. You will move forward with confidence because each step you take is influenced by your end goal. LinkedIn is a great place to start for most new users and you can build from there. Maybe you also want to learn about using YouTube to create educational videos. Or maybe you work with a product focused on women. It would make sense to spend time on Pinterest because it has a high percentage of female users. There isn't a right or wrong answer. Just go back to whether it will help the people you want to do business with to know, like, and trust you.

The pace of growth and change in social media isn't going to slow down anytime soon. The coronavirus pandemic accelerated the adoption of LinkedIn and other digital communication platforms, and the hybrid office/remote work of the future will hinge on our ability to connect online. So it's not going to pause to let you catch up. If you are overwhelmed now, well, it's just going to get worse. The best strategy is not to try to understand all the technology. Rather, know what you want to communicate to your audience, and use the appropriate tools to do that.

Use the technology to help people know, like, and trust you. Make it your friend, not your enemy.

Master Static and Active Strategies

When working with professionals on their LinkedIn strategies, the most common questions fall into two categories. First, they want to know how they should "show up." That really centers around the way they present themselves and the personal brand that we'll look at in the next section. But then the question comes around to what they should be *doing* on LinkedIn. What type of activities should they be doing on a day-to-day basis to make sure they are leveraging the platform. They say things like, "OK, fine, I gave up and got a LinkedIn profile. Now what do I actually do with it?"

These are important, but challenging, questions to answer because LinkedIn isn't a one-size-fits-all platform. Everyone will and should approach LinkedIn in a way that supports their overall business goals. And that will vary. Asking what to do with social media is like asking what you should do with email. It's simply another communication tool you can use to engage and interact with your clients, prospects, and partners.

When looking at what you should do, it's important to understand that there are two main areas of social media use: static and dynamic.

It's critical that you balance your focus in both of these areas. You can't do one and forget about the other. It's like a basketball coach would say, "You have to play both sides of the ball – defense and offense."

> *It's important to understand that there are two main areas of social media use: static and dynamic.*

Playing defense on social media means that you focus on the static content you create. You could consider it "passive" because it waits for your network to consume it on its own schedule. And even though you put effort into creating it, once you've shared this static content, it's up and doesn't require constant engagement. This works because the internet provides an information source that's open 24/7. The people looking you up might be potential clients, colleagues, or partners. Think about the last purchase you made or the last service provider you hired. I'm sure that you did your due diligence before you went forward. Your prospective connections are doing the same thing.

This is why it is so important to create an optimized LinkedIn presence – this is your static presence. People are looking for, and finding, information about you without you even knowing. And they are looking for you whether you like it or not. You want to ensure that you are sharing the message that you want them to find. Your LinkedIn profiles, both individual and company, are a key component of this presence. As is the content that you share with your network. When you first share it, it works more like the dynamic content we'll look at next. But when you add all of that content up over time, it acts like a trail of breadcrumbs describing your brand and what you focus on. And this plugs into your entire online ecosystem: your organization's website, other social media profiles, and other online content such as a blog or YouTube channel. Your network can consume all of this on its own schedule.

Playing offense on social media is a little bit of a misnomer. You certainly don't want to be offensive on social media! However, you do want to engage in activity that connects you with your network. This is the dynamic part of social media. Being active on social is about developing a dialogue between you and your network. This is an extension of the conversations you are having in the offline world. You can share ideas, answer questions, and build trust just like you would in the "real" world. And online conversations can be much more efficient and scalable.

LinkedIn gives you many ways to actively engage with your network. Of course, you can create and share content. You can also comment on and "like" the posts from your network. You can use the search features to find potential clients or partners. Or you could use the Groups or the hashtag function to find colleagues and peers who are having conversations about professional topics that are important to you. These are the activities that require you to be present consistently and regularly on LinkedIn for success.

Even though there isn't one perfect LinkedIn approach, an effective one will consist of both static and dynamic strategies. Michael Jordan is considered one of the best basketball players to play in the NBA. He could do amazing things as far as scoring points (he had the highest scoring average in NBA history). Many people forget, however, that a key to his success was that he was also a dominant defensive player. He could play both sides of the ball. You don't have to fly through the air to be successful. But if you want LinkedIn to be an effective part of your business, make online tools part of your daily activity.

1.6

Be On LinkedIn...But Don't Waste Time

The rise of social media platforms has been both a blessing and a curse. There is a host of new opportunities to create meaningful engagement in our personal and professional lives. We can have conversations at any time with people around the world. And at the same time, we can lose hours of productivity as we have conversations with people around the world (or just look at kitten videos). When we look at whether social media helps or hurts our productivity, we have to recognize that it gives options for connecting at the same time that it can become a major time suck. It really comes down to how you use it.

For example, my wife surfs Facebook after a long day to connect with her friends and see what people have posted. I play video games. Both are totally valid forms of relaxation. But I don't play video games in the middle of the day. And you shouldn't mindlessly surf LinkedIn and pretend that you are working.

It's important that you are deliberate and intentional with your work time on social media platforms. Here are ways that you can be more effective with your professional online activity.

1. Schedule your work and set a timer.

Before clicking on LinkedIn, map out your goals. Know how much time you are going to spend there and what activities you are going to do while there. That way you'll have a guidepost to focus your activity. And more importantly, you'll know when you are done and should log off.

2. Don't go on social media when you don't need to.

Digital platforms have given us an amazing ability to connect in ways that we haven't had before. But that doesn't mean that all our work needs to involve LinkedIn. Know when it's time to connect, comment, or collaborate, and when it's time to put your head down and do your work.

3. Turn off your notifications.

Every moment you aren't using their social media platforms, companies can't sell your attention to advertisers. Luckily for them, we give them permission to keep tempting us back by turning on our notifications. Every little "ding" calls us back like the Sirens called Odysseus. Unless your job is to directly monitor an account for possible negative activities, there aren't any emergencies on social media that you need to respond to immediately. Turn off your mobile and desktop notifications.

4. Create opportunities for self-awareness.

Get in the habit of asking yourself, "Do I really need to spend my time doing what I'm doing now? Is there a real professional reason for me to be here?" If the answer is no, move on to something else. That's why setting a timer to remind yourself to reassess is a good idea if you find your social media sessions stretching too long.

Should You Pay for LinkedIn?

A common question about LinkedIn is, "Should I pay to upgrade? Should I get the Premium LinkedIn account or buy a subscription to Sales Navigator?"

It's a great question. And one that doesn't necessarily have a clear-cut answer. I don't work for LinkedIn and I don't own Microsoft stock, so I don't have a vested interest in someone anteing up for the paid accounts. On the other hand, I do want you to get the biggest bang for your LinkedIn buck. And so I think it makes sense to use the platform as much as possible to move towards your business goals. But in the end, my answer is usually some variation of, "Yes. *Eventually.*"

Let me tell you why you shouldn't upgrade your account: Because you think that doing so will make your LinkedIn presence more effective without any additional work.

It's an easy mental trap to get caught in. Many professionals aren't completely comfortable with social media for business. People hope that by paying for LinkedIn it will somehow magically work better. The thinking goes something like, "It's hard to believe that LinkedIn can offer their really fantastic tools for free, so the good stuff must be in the premium account! That's how I'll get more engagement, build my network, and find more clients!" Too many professionals think that the secret to using LinkedIn is behind the magic curtain of a paid account (and LinkedIn's marketing department is happy to help them think that). But then they sign up, start paying...and nothing different happens.

While the premium account does give access to some very powerful features (more about that in a second), it doesn't do any of the work for you. You can have a premium account and still have no idea how to use LinkedIn effectively. Having access to these features doesn't guarantee success in itself. You still need to approach these features strategically and execute on a tactical level.

If you want to get the most out of the advanced features that the paid accounts provide, you need to start by maximizing the capabilities in your free account. Everything that we cover in this book is available through the free membership. You can optimize your profile, build a large network, and share content all without paying a dime. And you can be very successful doing so. While there isn't a "perfect" time to upgrade to a premium account, a few minutes of honest analysis will probably let you know where you are with your LinkedIn use. Just like a new piece of exercise equipment won't do your workouts for you, the paid features aren't going to connect and network for you. The paid versions of LinkedIn, while incredibly useful, aren't the magic pill for your LinkedIn results. You and your efforts are still going to be the driving force behind its value.

> *If you want to get the most out of the advanced features that the paid accounts provide, you need to start by maximizing the capabilities in your free account.*

The key is to maximize the use of the free features until you are being held back by the limits of the basic account. This is the best time to upgrade to the premium account: when you have bumped up against the ceiling of what you can do with the free account. If you've been using LinkedIn a lot, and you get irritated that you can't do more, that's the time to upgrade. You know that you're using all the available opportunities, and you want to open the net a bit and gain access to additional functions. (see 1.7.1)

For example, you might want to find more prospective connections or get a better sense of who is visiting your profile. Those are both examples where the paid subscriptions can help. For example, they allow access to fantastic tools like including an expanded "Who's Viewed Your Profile" section and additional search filters. (see 1.7.2) Those allow you to track your activity and visitors to uncover prospects and other business opportunities. You can also get access to LinkedIn Inmails through the paid accounts that allow you to reach out beyond your immediate network. You can view a full list of the premium features on LinkedIn's site (it does evolve and change). LinkedIn isn't foolish. If it has an incredibly useful feature that they think people will pay for, they are going charge users!

But the foundation you create and the active engagement you bring to your LinkedIn use will always be key to your success with the platform. Don't put the cart before the horse. Your success with the Premium or Sales Navigator account will be based on what you do with them. They are powerful tools, but even the best tool won't help if it's left in the drawer. You have to use it to get the true benefits of it.

Use Your LinkedIn Privacy Settings

O ne of the most powerful and (and probably least used) pages on LinkedIn is the **Privacy & Settings** section. (see 1.8.1 and 1.8.2) Privacy is a complex topic, and as a concept it's in flux right now. No matter what your personal approach to the information you share with the world at large, though, the ability to navigate the various privacy settings online is important. The LinkedIn settings for what information you share, where you share it, and how the platform engages with you are constantly evolving. In fact, I have often pointed to this section during live trainings and coaching sessions and found they have changed it overnight.

So the first piece of advice I can give you is to visit the Privacy & Settings page and spend 10 minutes going through it. There are over 75 options/switches to toggle in your Privacy and Setting section so writing about each of them would take its own separate book. Simply taking a few minutes to scroll down through the options will give you a much better sense of exactly what is being shared and seen through your account. And as we'll see, you don't have to tighten everything automatically. But you want to be knowledgeable about who in your network is seeing what, how LinkedIn is communicating with you, and what exactly they can do with your data.

Ultimately, what you decide to share and what you decide to keep private is largely dependent on your comfort level and on your goals for using LinkedIn. Focus on finding a balance between your privacy and security and being open to opportunity and connection. Networking, and by extension LinkedIn, works because it fosters new relationships. You can't do that if you don't share information. That would be like going to a networking event or conference and refusing to talk to anyone.

As the site and its functionality evolve, the exact methods for controlling what your network and the public can view will change, but there are a few key areas to pay attention to:

1. Who can see your profile and what can they see when they visit?

This is mostly controlled by the Public Profile setting, which allows you to hide part, or all, of your profile from being seen by non-connections. (see 1.8.3 and 1.8.4) You can also control how your profile headshot photo is displayed. In specific circumstances it can make sense to block certain information from being seen on your public profile, such as hiding the dates of your education/previous jobs if you are in a job search and are afraid of age discrimination. For most of us, however, it makes sense to allow your profile to be viewed by the public. Why spend time optimizing your profile if nobody sees it?

2. Who gets updates on your activity?

You can determine who sees changes made to your profile (like education updates or new jobs) in the How Others See Your Activity Section. You can also manage whether other LinkedIn members can see if you are active online. (see 1.8.5) Turning your activity broadcasts on and off can be useful when making a large number of changes to your profile. Turn it off as you are making the changes to prevent each one from popping up on your connections' newsfeeds. Switch it back on as you make the last change, and your connections will be alerted to your shiny new profile. Currently, it's also possible to determine who sees your individual posts on a post-by-post basis. (see 1.8.6)

Limiting the reach of your activity feed doesn't make a lot of sense if you are trying to share your brand with a wide audience. However, if you feel more comfortable sharing with those close to you, share your activity with only your direct connections or immediate network.

3. Who can see if you've visited their profile?

The "Who's Viewed Your Profile" feature gives you a list of those who have looked at your profile. It also lets the professionals you visit know that you have stopped by. (see 1.8.7) If you want to check out others anonymously, change Profile Viewing Options from your full information (name, picture, and headline) to the Private setting. If you are doing a lot of sales or recruitment prospecting, it can be helpful to go anonymous. However, if you are visiting profiles to get more information and possibly start a conversation, you should leave it open. It acts as a digital calling card and lets the other person know you care enough to do some pre-meeting research. Also, if your setting is on "Private" you won't be able to see who has viewed your profile.

LinkedIn likes to keep things fair. Balance your desire to stay hidden with the usefulness of seeing who is checking you out.

4. What is happening with your data?

Over the past few years, LinkedIn has responded to calls about data collection and data privacy by giving users more options for deciding how their data is being used by LinkedIn and third parties. By reviewing both the Data Privacy and Advertising Data sections on LinkedIn (see 1.8.8), you can see what information is public, see what information is being used and collected by LinkedIn to cater its advertising to you, and even download a copy of all of your data. Get in the habit of coming back to this section every few months to see if they've added new functionality and to review your existing settings. There isn't a right or wrong answer to how you manage these settings; it just has to be comfortable for you.

5. Who sees your email address?

Most professionals don't control their email addresses very well on LinkedIn. It's important because most have their primary email set to the personal address that they used when they first set up their account (and I've seen a lot of old ones like AOL and Hotmail). You can add multiple email addresses to your account in the Email Address section of Account Access. (see 1.8.9) I would suggest setting your work address as the primary address. This is the only one that the system will send emails to and that your LinkedIn connections can access. And you can control who sees that email, from only your first-level connections all the way up to every LinkedIn member.

Section 2

DEVELOP YOUR PERSONAL ONLINE BRAND

Your personal brand is how others perceive you as a professional. Whether you know it or not (and whether you like it or not), you already have a personal brand. When others think about you, they have a certain opinion of you. That's your brand. Or maybe other professionals don't think about you much. Unfortunately, that's your brand too!

It's impossible to control how others view us, but it is possible to influence their perceptions. The first step is to create clarity on how you want others to perceive you. What brand would encourage others to connect with you and engage with your message? When you know how you want others to see you, it will help inform all of your LinkedIn work. That brand message will determine everything from how you write your profile to your connection strategy to how you share content on LinkedIn.

2.1

What Is Your Personal Brand

Before we look at how to leverage LinkedIn for networking, we have to look at a very important, and often misunderstood concept: personal brand. There's a lot out of information out there about what a personal brand is, but let's keep it simple. Your personal brand is how people think about you when you aren't around. That's it. So when you are with a group of people, and you leave the room, the way they talk about you afterwards is connected to your brand.

> *Your personal brand is how people think about you when you aren't around.*

We've always had a personal brand; it's just that it didn't have a broad reach before easy access to communication tools like social media. But brand was a key element of professional networking and relationship-building even before the rise of digital communication. It was also an element that most professionals put little deliberate attention on, which was a huge mistake. Because you always had a brand. It was just a matter of whether you were developing and sharing it intentionally or by default.

And what digital communication, social media, and specifically for the professional space, LinkedIn, has provided is a forum to share that personal brand on a larger scale than ever before. The access that we have to eyeballs is orders of magnitude greater than it ever was. Before digital communication, your personal brand would only affect people that you physically ran into. You could only impact people when you are with them at work, at a conference, or other offline networking events. Now, you can engage with hundreds or thousands of professionals while on your commute (if you aren't driving) or while sitting at your desk. Even a LinkedIn post that is seen by only a few hundred people is still seen by *a few hundred people!*

As we cover the ways to share your message through LinkedIn, whether it's through your profile or through the content you share, it's important that we have a clear understanding of what that message is. The modern professional, no matter their job title, has a bit of a marketing role. And a fundamental principle in marketing is to have a clear, understandable message. You want to make sure that your audience can easily engage with what you are sharing and how you fit into their mental landscape. That's why it's so important that you start your LinkedIn journey by knowing what you are trying to say. You have to think strategically about your message before you can think about the tactics you are going to use to communicate it.

By being intentional about the brand message you want to share on LinkedIn, you can create some direction in your activities. You'll be more likely to influence your network the way you want to influence them.

2.2

Create Brand Through Visibility and Reputation

When it was common to work for the same company our entire careers, the idea of a personal brand wasn't that important. These days, the employment contract between employer and employee has changed a lot. Shorter job stints and a "free agent" economy where it's common for professionals to bounce from employer to employer mean that a strong brand is incredibly important. Even if you stay with the organization, your career advancement will be determined by how people view you. It's important that people know about you and know about your experience and capabilities.

But how do you manage your personal brand and still get everything done on your to-do list? Here comes social media and LinkedIn to the rescue. Your brand rests on how you are viewed by your network, i.e. the people that you know and the people that know you. And when you take all of those people in total, well, that parallels your LinkedIn network. That's why LinkedIn is such a powerful tool to develop and share your personal brand. There are two main components of your personal brand, and LinkedIn can have a huge impact on both.

The first is **visibility**. As our networks get bigger and as more information fights for people's attention, it can be harder to be seen. We don't always have the time to meet for a business lunch or go to a conference, and we might not have a close enough relationship to give people a call just to catch up. But by connecting with our network online, we are given permission to talk to them through LinkedIn. We are inviting them into our sphere of influence, and they are inviting us into theirs. Every time you show up on the newsfeed of your first-level connections, you get a visibility bump.

This isn't a new thing. It's called top of mind advertising and it accounts for a lot of the advertising you see on a daily basis. For example, Coca-Cola spends millions of dollars every year advertising a product that everyone already knows about. There is a reason for this. When you get thirsty, the first thing they want coming to your mind is "I want a Coke." They know that they are competing for your attention and want to make sure they are visible. When your network thinks about your field, specialty, or niche, the first thing you want them to think about is you! And with LinkedIn, you don't have to spend those millions of dollars.

How your network sees you is based on your **reputation**, which multiplies the power of visibility. It's not just how many times they see your name, but the ideas and emotions that get attached to your name when it's seen. Do they think you are competent, experienced, and connected? Or do they think the opposite? What are the areas of expertise that you can help them with? All of this is tied up with your reputation. If you are on your connections' minds when you aren't around, that's visibility. What they are saying about you when you aren't in the room – that's reputation. This is why being strategic about the content of your online activities is a valuable use of your time.

It's important to have a clear thread that connects your LinkedIn profile, your status updates, and all your online engagement. By reinforcing visibility and reputation on LinkedIn, you'll find benefits that reach well beyond your online activities. In the real world, your network will have a clearer idea about the problems you solve, and more and better opportunities will come your way. And that's when you'll know that your brand has value!

2.3

Your Brand Isn't Your Resume

When you get to its core, LinkedIn is a powerful site. You have a platform that allows you to share your professional story easily and at scale. Your posts allow you to share up-to-date information on your career. And your profile is a website that is all about you: your experiences, your skills, and your education. In other words: your story. But most of us aren't that experienced in telling (and writing) our story, so we get flustered when we are putting together our profile.

A common trap people fall into is approaching their LinkedIn presence like they would a resume. That makes sense, because LinkedIn started as a tool to help candidates connect with employers and vice versa. It's only in the last few years that more people have grasped the power of LinkedIn for engaging with each other professionally outside of a job search. And this was accelerated by the social distancing during the coronavirus pandemic. Unfortunately, though, one of the lingering negative effects of the recruiting/HR history of LinkedIn is that people still fall back on using resume-speak when crafting their brand on LinkedIn. Especially when looking at the LinkedIn profile section, it's common to see the jargon and empty phrases people use when putting together a resume.

The big problem with resume-speak is that no one believes it. So many resumes are full of cliches that people just gloss over them when they show up:

> *The big problem with resume-speak is that no one believes it.*

Results-driven…yeah, right.
Team-oriented…sure you are.
Goal-focused…if you say so.

These days, people are skeptical about what they read and hear. Whether it's an advertisement on TV, a marketing message online, or a resume, we've learned to tune out most of what people tell us. How can you share your awesomeness, then, if your audience won't believe what you tell them?

Don't *tell* people how good you are.

Show them.

Because of our innate skepticism to what we hear, we've learned to give a lot of credence to results and actions that can be seen and documented. That's why online content can be powerful: because it is chock-full of ways for you to demonstrate all the experiences, skills, and knowledge that you have. For example, when you are considering your overall strategy on LinkedIn, think of how your profile can show that you possess all the attributes you claim. And even your LinkedIn posts are a way to show your skills in action.

In other words, how can you prove that you can walk the walk and not just talk the talk? The goal is to make sure that your profile and activity are actively demonstrating your message, not just parroting some over-used cliches.

Here are a few places to start when looking for ways to show your story instead of just telling it.

1. Take as many adjectives as possible out of your profile.

Try this: Print out your profile onto a piece of paper. Take a pencil. Cross out all the adjectives. Is your profile still compelling? If not, you are leaning too heavily on using the adjectives to tell people about yourself. It would be hard to have a profile completely devoid of adjectives, but it's a great goal to have.

2. Use the additional information sections to tell your story.

The LinkedIn profile has several areas that allow you to go deeper into your story, so use them. If you are highly trained in your field, list your certifications or classes in the education section. Are you a thought leader in your industry? Then list the publications you have authored or that you have been mentioned in. If you network a lot or are involved in your community, be sure to list the groups that you are in. And be sure to list any volunteer work you do. It will humanize you and create a fuller picture of you as an individual.

3. Write for people.

Remember that the visitor to your profile is a person, not a search bot looking for keywords. Use language that is understandable to the average reader. Keep it simple and to the point!

Write Online Like You Speak Offline

There's a common mistake that professionals make when thinking about their personal brand. They get stuck thinking of it from their own point of view. And they end up making assumptions, using lots of jargon, and creating complicated ideas that only make sense in their own head.

I read a lot of LinkedIn profiles. I've seen great profiles that really let me know who a person is and what they are all about as a professional. And I've read profiles that...well, that leave me scratching my head. For example, this is a sentence that was really on a LinkedIn profile. (I've changed details to protect the uninformed.)

> "I enjoy vectoring in on product/marketing strategy and taking intelligent risks to further my company's mission. Constantly aspiring to work in an agile and effective manner across real and perceived functional boundaries to demonstrate leadership, leverage, and results."

What!?

Here's the deal. This person is highly capable, highly qualified, and successful. I've met them. But that doesn't come through at all because it's lost in jargon and business euphemisms. This happens frequently because of LinkedIn's roots in resumes and technical writing. Unfortunately, your readers don't want to slog through all that mumbo-jumbo to figure out what you actually do. They aren't looking for your autobiography. They want to know if you can help them with whatever problem they are trying to solve.

Here's my rule for online activity. I call it D. Fish's Axiom of Proper Language on Social Media Platforms:

"If you wouldn't say a sentence in the real world, don't write it in your digital communication."

That's it. When you are sharing your brand, double-check that you are being accessible. When you write something on your LinkedIn profile, say it out loud before you publish it. If it doesn't work when you say it, you should go back and rewrite what you just wrote. Make your profile clear, concise, and understandable. This applies to your posts and comments as well. Be a human being. Because if you force your reader to decipher what you have on your profile, no one will care if you are brilliant or not. They will have already stopped paying attention.

2.5

The 3 Questions That Drive Your LinkedIn Approach

At the root of every ineffective LinkedIn profile and wasted status update is a lack of planning and forethought. Even with over 700 million users (or maybe because it has over 700 million users), most people are still on LinkedIn in a reactive capacity. They created their profile because others invited them to connect or they just felt like they were "supposed to." If they post content it's because they heard it was important, but they aren't sure why. In fact, less than 1% of LinkedIn members actively post content and that's because most haven't thought about how it could benefit their careers. They don't know how LinkedIn fits strategically into their professional goals. And they don't know how to approach it in a way that will enable them to leverage their time. They haven't thought through what they are trying to accomplish and therefore they accomplish very little.

Asking and answering a few simple strategic questions can go a long way to making your LinkedIn experience much easier, more effective, and more efficient. It's important to know what you are trying to say before you look at the ways that you can say it. A clear focus is the biggest differentiator between a good and bad online presence. These questions are the foundation for all your LinkedIn activity, and in some ways, all of your professional online activity. They give you a litmus test that you can use to decide what to do on LinkedIn and how to go about doing it.

> *Asking and answering a few simple strategic questions can go a long way to making your LinkedIn experience much easier, more effective, and more efficient.*

Before you work through your profile, post content, and engage with your network on LinkedIn, there are three important questions to examine.

1. What are your most important business goals?

It's important for you to articulate the goals that you are working towards in your career. Can you clearly spell them out? Though they may seem obvious to you, if they remain vague ideas, then you will struggle to communicate them. It's not enough to say, "I am trying to advance in my company." Or "I want to get more clients." Be exact. Write the answer down. You'll find that in doing so you take the fuzzy ideas in your head and make them concrete.

It doesn't have to be complex. It can be as simple as saying, "I want to develop relationships with the leadership in my company so that I can get a promotion in the next 12 months." If you are in sales you could say, "I want to increase my pipeline of high-level prospects so that I can close five additional deals this quarter." Looking for a new position? How about, "I want to increase my visibility as an expert in my field, which will enable me to get three job offers."

2. Who is the most important audience for you to communicate with?

There will be many different people viewing your profile. If you try to speak to all of them at the same time, your message will be very muddled. Identify the most useful group that will see your message. In marketing, this is often called your "buyer persona." It's a way to describe the ideal recipient of your message. Your profile and content should focus on this group.

That doesn't mean you should exclude everyone else outside your target audience, but they will understand your message (and who it is for) if you are clear enough. For example, executives who focus on the decision-makers at their client companies will still be understandable to their peers and other industry professionals. Those "third-party observers" will realize the main intent of the message and still get valuable context.

3. What message does that audience need to hear?

Once you know exactly who is in your target audience, consider what they need to hear from you. The best communicators focus on the information their audience needs to receive, not just on what they want to say. This is the core of your personal brand. Understanding how you want to be perceived is a critical step towards sharing effectively on LinkedIn.

If you are struggling with this, pretend that your ideal profile visitor is physically with you. Maybe they're sitting across the table or you are talking to them at an event. What would you say to them? What would you want them to know about you? Would you highlight your experience, your passion, your unique ability to solve their problems, or something different? This will give you the foundation for building your brand message.

These three steps create the strategic underpinnings of an effective LinkedIn presence. When faced with questions about what to write on your profile or share with your network, go back to these answers. They will point you in the right direction by creating a focus point for your activity. As your career evolves, so will the answers to these questions. It can be useful to come back to this exercise every once in a while to update and refine your answers. But by creating this clarity in the present, the tactical decisions you need to make daily become that much simpler.

Define Your Online Audience Clearly

'm going to let you eavesdrop on a conversation I've had with hundreds of people while talking about networking and their LinkedIn presence:

> Me: *"So who is your target audience? Who's the group you want to engage and work with?"*

> Well-Meaning Professional: *"Everyone! Which is why I'm totally confused about why I don't have more opportunities!"*

It's sad but true that I usually have this conversation with professionals who are struggling to find success in their chosen field. It's ironic, but whether they are a small business owner, a salesperson, or an executive for a large company, someone who thinks that everyone is their customer is usually short of customers.

Someone who thinks that everyone is their customer is usually short of customers.

In the last section, we looked at the three questions that should guide your LinkedIn strategy. And one of those is specifically focused on your target audience. And like any target, the more clearly you've defined where you are aiming, the more likely you are to hit it. That's why professionals who are keeping their options open are actually hurting themselves. In reality, they haven't put the time and effort into defining who they serve. Or they are afraid of committing to a specific demographic and cutting themselves off from future opportunities. By doing so, they make themselves an unmemorable commodity to their prospects, clients, and peers. If you know economics, you know that a commodity's price falls to the lowest point possible to barely cover costs. That "low-value" place is not where you want to be.

Lots of great things happen when you have a clearly defined audience that you serve. Most importantly, you can communicate more clearly to partners and clients because you have articulated the exact problems you solve. Your personal branding becomes more effective because it speaks to specific needs and specific customers. Also, others can refer you more easily because they can grasp what you do, and they'll know where you fit into the spectrum of your field. Yes, the people who are outside of your target market are less likely to respond, but it's offset by the fact that your ideal clientele will know how to find you.

Here's a slightly morbid example, but one that illustrates the point well:

- If you're a general practice doctor, you compete against every other doctor, health clinic, and webmd.com for patients (i.e. clients).

- If you are an oncologist, people who have cancer will work harder to find you because you focus on the solutions to their specific problem.

- If you're an oncologist who specializes in pancreatic cancer, the pool of people who need your expertise is smaller. But if they have pancreatic cancer, they are really motivated to find you.

- And if you are the oncologist who is the expert in a rare type of pancreatic cancer that only affects one hundred people a year, you best believe most of those one hundred people will seek out your services.

Plant a flag. Narrow your focus to a specific group that you can help more effectively than anyone else. Then tell everyone.

2.7

Choose Your Themes to Focus On

t's also important to decide what you are going to talk about on LinkedIn to create the biggest impact. When you define your target audience, you can narrow your focus to the topics that are going to be relevant to them.

The easiest way to create a strategy around your content is to consider the different themes that your profile and posts are going to highlight. These are areas that you are going to consistently focus on so that you will position yourself as a knowledgeable resource and valuable connection in the minds of your network. You can think of them as the tactical representation of your brand strategy. Because what you talk about matters.

You don't have to limit yourself to only one theme, but you want to keep it to between three and five. Just like a very clear business niche will make it easier for your network to understand who you work with, having a tight focus on the themes you discuss will allow people to easily understand what you do, who you work with, and the problems you solve.

Professional Themes:

You might think that everything you post on LinkedIn is contained within the "professional" theme, but we're focused here on topics that are specific to the work you do daily. The areas you discuss in the Professional theme should revolve around the services you provide for the people you work with. That might be external clients and customers or your internal colleagues that you support. For example, if you are in sales you can talk about your products and services and how they help the end-user. If you are in marketing: specific channels like digital, graphic design, SEO, or strategy. Or if you are in software engineering you could discuss the types of projects you work on and the platforms and languages you regularly work in.

Industry/Field Themes:

Taking a step up from the day-to-day work, you can also contribute to larger conversations happening within your profession. These could be discussions about best practices or trends that are transforming the industry. Topics could be anything from business development and digital transformation to client benefits or new products types. The key here is to pick areas that you are knowledgeable and interested in. If you don't feel a topic is relevant or engaging for you, don't talk about it. But if it's something that impacts you and that you have an opinion about, be sure to comment.

Work/Career Themes:

Regardless of the work you do, there are high-level conversations about how work impacts our lives, and vice-versa. These can range from work/

life balance and mental health to sustainability and diversity/inclusion. Again, the goal is not to address every possible topic. Choose an area that you are engaged in offline and bring that to your online engagement. For example, if you are an entrepreneur who is navigating the new work-from-anywhere landscape for you and your remote team, you can bring that into your LinkedIn brand. Or if your employer is committed to sustainability and you think that's important, talk about it.

Profersonal™ Themes:

While LinkedIn is a professional platform, a lot of our professional interactions involve an element of the personal. That's why my friend Jason Seiden first coined the term *profersonal*™ to label the human-to-human conversations that happen in professional settings, especially online. This isn't strictly an online concept. Think of the conferences and professional events you attend. As you get to know people there, your conversations probably encompass your personal lives as well as professional topics.

The key is to remember that context is important. While you can and should share a bit of your personal life on LinkedIn, remember that you are still in a professional setting. You don't have to share private information, but if you have something that takes up a lot of your time in the offline world, there's nothing wrong with sharing it online. I have connections who share occasional updates about their favorite hobbies (competition-level barbeque, powerlifting), nonprofit involvement (Special Olympics, Habitat for Humanity), and travels (trekking through Southeast Asia).

2.8

Incorporate Side Hustles into Your Personal Brand

These days it's common for professionals to have side hustles. These could be part-time jobs, hobbies that bring in an income, passion projects, or other supplemental gigs. Maybe they do it because they want to bring in some extra money, or maybe they are toying around with starting their own business someday. Or maybe they just really love doing something beyond their regular 9-5.

No matter the reasons, these activities are an integral part of people's lives, so how should we account for them in our online presence? I get asked all the time about whether these side hustles belong on someone's LinkedIn profile. And the answer I usually give is:

"Maybe, but you have to be very careful how you do it. And if in doubt, don't."

When visitors are reading your profile, they don't know much, if anything, about you beyond what they read. That's why it's so important to be clear and concise when sharing your message. If it's broad and rambling they won't know how to pull out the most important threads. Every additional piece you add to your story can muddy the waters. When you share a side gig or outside passion on your profile, you could be creating a mixed message. From your perspective, you are just trying to provide a richer picture of yourself. But they could interpret this as split interests. This can detract from your professional credibility in their eyes.

For example, if you were going to hire a plumber to fix your toilet, would you want to hire one who spent all their energy focused on pipes or one who also played jazz piano? While the music probably doesn't take away from someone's wrench skills, if you had a choice between the two, wouldn't you want to hire the one who solely focuses on your plumbing?

Should you always avoid mentioning your extracurricular activities? Of course not. But be sure it fits with the overall message you want to send. Part of this will depend on how much time and energy this side gig requires. I know a successful business owner who is an assistant football coach at his old high school. He played in high school and college, and he wanted to stay connected with his alma mater and the kids. It takes up some of his time during the season, but that's all. No one thinks that he is going to start coaching in the NFL anytime soon, so he put it on his profile as a hobby. In fact, it helps him start conversations with people because they see it and ask him how the season is shaping up.

If you look at my LinkedIn profile, you will see I used to play drums in a band. It helps to explain why my company is called RockStar and why I still use the nickname I earned on the stage. But I also make it clear that it was in the past and that my focus now is on my speaking and coaching. It spurs a lot of conversations about music and drumming, and that fits with my overall brand. It also explains why I use so many music metaphors when I am on stage.

That works if your side job is more of a hobby or in the past, but what if your side hustle is a big part of what you do in the present? I know someone who runs a social media agency and at the same time is an incredibly active fitness instructor. For her, teaching fitness is a central activity to who she is as a person and a professional. She combines the two online brands by talking about the power of taking action on the right activities to create success on social media as well as your personal health. In her view, for both a business using social media or an individual pursuing physical fitness, the same rules apply. She's created a unified story, and thus an aligned brand, where success online and at the gym stem from the same processes.

As more and more professionals pursue side gigs, we'll get more comfortable sharing and understanding the nuances and wrinkles in our and in others' careers. That might take a little while, though. In the meantime, you don't have to hide or avoid your other interests and passions. But it's usually best not to lead with them. Weave your side work into the story of who you are as a professional.

The goal is to create a larger umbrella narrative that fits all your activity. Taking the opportunity to humanize yourself and provide some depth is fantastic. But remember that the reader is still creating an initial impression. If your side activity is too tangential, it's OK to leave it off. If there is a way to integrate your side activity into your main message, go for it.

2.9

The Key to Sharing in a Short-Attention-Span World

Fifteen seconds.

By the end of those few seconds, over half of a webpage's visitors have left (according to research by digital metric tracker Chartbeat in 2014). And if you do a quick Google search on "how long do viewers stay on a webpage," you'll find a host of other stats, numbers, and figures, but they all point to a simple fact:

People don't spend a lot of time reading online information.

This has important ramifications for your online presence, especially with your social media profiles and posts. When a prospective client or other interested party visits, they are looking for more information on you. However, they aren't looking for an autobiography. You have only moments to communicate your message and engage them. Because of this, you want to think like a journalist and focus on your critical messages. It's counter-intuitive, but to effectively snag your visitors in that window you should realize that less can be more. Focus on short, powerful, and clear messages instead of overwhelming them with a large amount of information. In this situation, quality is much more important than quantity.

> *Focus on short, powerful, and clear messages instead of overwhelming the reader with a large amount of information.*

That is a challenge for many professionals, who are trained to be incredibly thorough when communicating the facts and figures of what they do. (Think about the last PowerPoint presentation you saw.) We're taught to cover everything and so we're afraid of leaving out important facts or over-simplifying. Because it is so easy to continue to add content, we think that we should dump as much information as possible into our online presence.

Remember that a short attention span does not equal stupidity. When talking about online attention spans with many veteran professionals, I've encountered a dismissive attitude among many of them. They want to complain that the shorter attention spans of online visitors point to a lack of intelligence, sophistication, or decision-making ability. This attitude is reinforced when it is lumped together with complaints about the "younger generation."

But that's often the exact opposite of what is happening. If you haven't noticed, we live in a world with a glut of information, and we need to process it quickly. If you were a digital native who grew up in a world overloaded with information, wouldn't you process information quickly as well? You'd want to make sure that you weren't wasting your time. And it's not just young people; it applies to all generations. It's important to keep in mind that your online presence, especially your LinkedIn profile and posts, aren't meant to be fully representative. They aren't full conversations. Instead, you are offering an introduction so they can choose whether to engage with you further.

Studies done by Microsoft also show that if someone does stay on a website for longer than 15 seconds, the likelihood that they'll stay increases. Basically, you have a few seconds to make a good first impression. And if you do make a good first impression and create value, people will give you more time. So make sure that you are starting with a clear, impactful message on your profile and in your posts. And allow the reader to opt-in to you so they'll spend more time with you online. In this way, short attention spans are a way of vetting an information source to make sure it's valuable and useful.

What is the first impression that your profile visitors and content readers have? When people see your online content, they will make judgments in just moments based on these few pieces of information. They won't even do it consciously. Act like a journalist and create a strong lead. Whether it's the images and headlines on your profile or the first few lines of a post, consider how someone will spend those first few moments. Will they encourage people to opt-in and go further, or will it push them away.

By the way, before we bemoan the short attention span of the next generation, keep in mind that it's all relative. An ancient Greek who was listening to the *Iliad* (remember, they were an illiterate culture) would need more than a few seconds or minutes. It would take about 15 hours! If you had asked them, we've been living in a short-attention-span world for a long time.

It's too late to debate the positive and negative aspects of a short-attention-span culture. It's already here. If you are going to be successful in this new world, it's important to position yourself in a way people can understand and digest. Remember, once you've engaged your online visitors, they've made an important decision to give you some of their attention (which is a very scarce resource). Once that has happened, you can dive deeper into the complexities and nuances of how you help. But don't put the cart before the horse!

Section 3

CRAFT A ROCKSTAR LINKEDIN PROFILE

For modern professionals, the LinkedIn profile is one of the main pillars of their online professional presence. In fact, for many professionals, it is *the* main tool to communicate with everyone from colleagues and partners to clients and prospective employers. A quick Google search of someone's name and city often puts their LinkedIn profile page at the top of the search results.

Too often, professionals look at the blanks on their LinkedIn profile and start filling them in with little pre-planning. And then they wonder why they don't get good results! The personal branding strategy that you developed in the previous section will guide what you put on the page (or screen as it were) as you craft your LinkedIn profile. You don't have to be a professional writer or marketer to have a great profile. It's simply a matter of taking each piece in turn and using it as a tool to communicate your professional brand story. Let's make sure it's saying the right things!

3.1

Write a First-Person Profile

One question that is disarmingly simple centers on the voice you should use in your profile. Should you use the first-person or the third-person voice when crafting your message? Should you use "I, me, and my" or should you use your name? This is especially important to consider for the About and Experience sections. Those are open fields where you can communicate directly with your reader.

In the early, Wild West days of LinkedIn, I said that either direction was fine. But as the platform has evolved, it's become clear that the first-person profile is the way to go. If you write in the third-person, two negative thoughts pop up in the mind of your reader. First, they start to doubt whether you wrote it, or if someone else did. There's a short mental jump from there to doubting the credibility of the message. Secondly, it makes you sound like a pompous ass. Would you ever speak of yourself in the third-person when talking to someone in the offline world?

There's an underlying assumption that each person writes their own profile. And even if they get help (I've helped thousands of professionals craft their profiles), it should come from their voice. The profile isn't the same as a bio page found on a company website. The profile should be an extension of what you would tell someone if you met them in the offline world. In fact, if you aren't comfortable writing about yourself, it can help to imagine that you are speaking to your visitor at a professional event when you're writing these sections. You can even start each paragraph with the word "I."

Your visitor wants to read about your career and professional life from your perspective. Speak from that perspective and share a message that connects with your reader's needs.

3.2

Use Banner Image Wisely

H umans are wired for sight. Literally. We have over 30,000 nerve receptors in our ears but over 1 million in our eyes. When we have an opportunity to communicate visually, we need to take advantage of it.

Ironically, LinkedIn was resistant to visual storytelling for a long time. While platforms like Instagram and Pinterest are almost based entirely on pictures, LinkedIn has only started to position video and images more prominently. For a long time, there was only one image attached to your profile, your headshot. As the platform added multimedia to the different sections, it was possible to cheat a little to add more images to your profile. You could use the thumbnails of videos, slideshows, and .pdf files to share more visual information in the profile. And that's still a valid way to get more images into your profile. But these were ad hoc fixes.

That's why the relatively recent addition of the Profile Banner photo is a big deal. (see 3.2.1) It has been the first meaningful visual component added to the LinkedIn profile since the beginning. It's effectively doubled the number of images that you can add to the

Header section of your LinkedIn Profile. And the banner has a lot more open space that you can use to share information. (Currently, LinkedIn recommends a 1584 x 366 image for the banner.) That's significantly more than just your small headshot.

The banner also allows for more expression because it doesn't have to be a headshot of you. It could be almost anything! But that doesn't mean that it should be. Stay focused. Your banner image selection should have one overarching goal: set a tone. You want to help set your reader's expectations. And that will influence how they read the rest of your profile.

Even before they start reading, your banner and headshot are going to influence how they feel about your credibility, accessibility, and likeability. They are going to make these decisions unconsciously and without even trying. It's just like meeting someone in real life. Even before we start talking, we take in visual cues like their attire and facial expressions to judge how we should interact. We don't do this intentionally. This is simply how our brains are wired for interpersonal communication.

> *Even before they start reading, your banner and headshot are going to influence how they feel about your credibility, accessibility, and likeability.*

That's why it's important that we are deliberate with what we share on our Banner. It's not enough to just have a pretty picture. And don't use an image just because you think it looks cool. This is the first opportunity to communicate with your visitors. You don't want to miss out on the chance to share your message, or worse, confuse them. You want to align your image with the overall theme of your profile.

Some ideas of banner images that set a tone:

- A branded image from your organization. It could be just a company logo or a photo from your marketing material that includes logos, brand colors, or other taglines.
- A photo of your team taken at an event, like a conference, celebration, or even a party at the office.
- An image that features the accomplishments of you or your organization, for example industry awards, a book, or product that you created.
- An action shot of you doing the work you do.
- If your work centers around a specific location – like a city, building, or school – use a photo to let people know.

These are just a few of the ideas on how to use the banner image. The key is to be intentional with the message that you are sending to your visitor.

3.3

Pick the Right Headshot Photo

They say a picture is worth a thousand words. So what are the thousand words that your profile headshot is saying about you? Is it aligned with the message that you want to share through your profile? People like to "see" who they are interacting with. YouTube has hundreds of hours of video uploaded every minute, and one of the most popular social media sites right now is the photo site Instagram. It's common for people to say, "I can't remember people's names, but I can always remember a face." That visual preference has followed us online.

Besides your banner image, your headshot is the only photo attached to every profile. That is why it plays such an important role. (see 3.3.1) On LinkedIn, a profile with a photo gets approximately 11 times more traction than a profile without a photo. These days, a profile with the empty outline indicating that you haven't uploaded a photo makes you a bit of a non-entity. (see 3.3.2) Used correctly, a good headshot captures the message that you share on your profile and represents it visually. Another way of thinking about this: You wouldn't go to a networking event with a paper bag over your head, would you?

The first rule of thumb with your headshot is to keep the photo consistent with the rest of the information you are sharing. Ask yourself, "Does the person in the photo resemble the same person that the visitor is reading about?" If you talk about how hard you work for your customers, but your photo is you lounging on a beach, there's a mismatch. Similarly, if you're sharing your many successes on your profile, but the photo is a blurry selfie taken with a cell phone camera, your audience will wonder just how successful you really are.

> *To be effective, your LinkedIn headshot photo should be consistent, polished, and approachable.*

This highlights the need to be polished in your photo. Both you, and the photo itself, need to have a certain degree of professional polish. You don't need an uptight headshot, but you should convey that others can trust your competence. The prevalence of good cameras means that we expect to see high-quality photos, so don't short-change yourself. Low-grade or inappropriate photos make your visitors doubt the professionalism of the person in the photo. Adding a bit of polish to the picture is also driven by the context of the photo: what you are wearing and the background of the photo. Dress for success and be aware of your surroundings.

Balance that polish with approachability. Humanize yourself. Your facial expression conveys how approachable you are (or aren't). Would your reader feel comfortable interacting with the person in your headshot in the offline world? Is it open, warm, and friendly? Can your visitor imagine starting a conversation with you if they met you at a business meeting? Your profile visitor is asking themselves how they should engage with you, and an approachable photo lets them feel comfortable taking the next step.

Selecting a great photo is easier than we make it out to be. It's normal for us to look at our own photos and see the tiny imperfections. But the goal isn't to have a photo for the next cover of *GQ* or *Vogue*. We're trying to convey information about us as professionals to our profile visitors. Everyone else looks at your photo and (usually subconsciously) mines it for contextual information: "Where is this person?" "What message does their clothing send?" "Are they smiling at me and therefore friendly?"

These are the same thoughts that go through our head when we meet someone in person. The advantage we have online is that we can strategically choose the photo that will send the message that we want. If you are struggling to choose the right photo, ask for an outside perspective. Send three photos to a few close friends and see which one they like. There are also online sites that allow you to post photos for assessment by others.

A few quick guidelines: Make the photo of you and just you. Keep other people (and your fishing trophy) out. Position the photo well so that you are centered and zoom in close enough that it's easy to see your face (but not so close that you are cutting off parts of your head or hair). Only use action shots if they coincide with your work. For example, if you speak at a lot of meetings, then a picture of you presenting could work. And finally, though it may seem obvious, make sure that it's a photo that looks like you. Your online presence needs to support your offline activities. If the person in the photo doesn't look like you, or if he or she looks like the "you" of ten years ago, then it's not doing its job.

Put the same care in managing your online appearance as your offline appearance and you'll be fine.

3.4

Start Your Profile with a Reader-First Headline

Headlines are important. Whether it's a newspaper, a blog article, or your LinkedIn profile, the headline performs a number of important tasks. (see 3.5.1)

First, it grabs attention. Newspapers have huge front-page headlines because they want to snag the attention of people walking by the newsstand. Because there are so many messages bombarding us daily, it's critical to cut through the noise. In the same way, your profile headline should reach out to hook your ideal audience. This is doubly important because the information that appears in LinkedIn Search results includes your name, picture, and *headline*. You want it to grab the reader.

Secondly, you want to give the reader the opportunity to opt-in to you. Eye-tracking studies show that people spend more time on average reading the headline than any other part of the profile. They are processing the information and deciding whether it's worth reading more. Since time is such a valuable commodity, they are vetting you based on the information you share in the headline.

Finally, the headline creates a framework for the reader of your profile. They will know what to expect based on how you start the profile. A blog article that starts with the headline "5 Ways to Improve Your LinkedIn Headlines" leads to the expectation of exactly five ideas for your online social profile. In the same way, your headline lets the reader know what they will find in the profile that follows.

How do you construct a headline that does all of that? The goal is to focus on making it compelling and informational like a newspaper headline. By the way, I said newspaper headline, not a tabloid headline. It's not about shouting, but rather telling your reader who you help and how you help them.

The default setting of the headline is your current position and company, which is pulled from your Experience section. If you listed Project Manager at Company XYZ as your current position, that's your default headline. It is important to realize that your job title may or may not be meaningful to your outside reader. As you go up the company hierarchy, job titles have more resonance outside the organization. For example, everyone knows what a CEO does. But what if you are a salesperson, account representative, director, or small business owner? You can't assume that every reader has access to your job description and there's very little information in those titles for an outside reader. Right now, there are over 1.6 million "account executives" on LinkedIn. They work for a wide variety of companies with a wide variety of responsibilities. In that situation, you couldn't rely on your job title to communicate your value and your areas of expertise to your reader.

The solution is to take a cue from the search engine optimization world. Focus on populating your headline with keywords that describe your target audience or the challenges that you solve for your target audience. The keywords that you select in this scenario won't be determined by a computer search algorithm. Instead, let your selection process be guided by words that your ideal audience will respond to.

This is another reason why knowing your ideal audience is important. You want your headline to resonate with your target market when they first see it.

A simple way to add these keywords is in two areas: who you help and what you help them with. In fact, a useful template for brainstorming the headline is:

"Helping (insert who you help) with (what you help them with)"

This allows your visitor to think "I'm looking at the right person" when they see your profile. It also stands out more in the search results. Instead of having a dry job title, your target audience will see something that resonates with them. It could be:

- Helping Fortune 500 Companies Solve Complex Personnel Issues
- Helping Medical Professionals Manage and Grow Wealth
- Helping Our Sales Team Deliver Amazing Customer Experiences

You can easily use a different verb than "helping." It's simply a starting point for our brainstorming. However, it's effective because your profile visitors are looking for help and we want to be as direct as possible.

Crafted properly, your headline will serve as a beacon to the audience that you want to talk to. It creates a positive first impression and draws them in to find out more about you.

3.5

Words to Avoid in Your Headline

Over the years, I've seen a lot of LinkedIn profiles and a lot of headlines. This means I've seen the good, the bad, and the downright ugly of social media.

And I've compiled a list of what you want to stay away from when talking about yourself on LinkedIn. Too often, professionals try to be cute or clever, and it just comes off as foolish, arrogant, or clueless. Or they use terms that they think are informative that are really bland and meaningless. Instead, just focus on being clear. Here's a list of words that hurt your ability to communicate and engage with your network.

1. Ninja

No. You're not. Just no. Stop it.

2. Guru

Are you going to be a spiritual guide to website marketing or graphic design or whatever? Why not just call yourself the high priest, pope, or cult leader? That would look foolish and so does using guru. You're attempting to gain credibility by attaching yourself to a system of spirituality that you know nothing about. You look foolish, and nobody trusts gurus anyways.

3. Account Executive

If you have a common/generic job title, it's not going to help others understand why they should engage with you. Your readers have no idea what it means in your specific situation. Please, take two minutes to write something more descriptive. Use the keywords-driven approach I shared in the last chapter instead of just your job title.

4. Founder

This one's tough, because if you are a founder, your life is wrapped up in the business you created and it demonstrates a level of expertise. But your reader doesn't care about your story; they care about how you can help them. And founder really doesn't tell them how you help… unless you founded Uber or Twitter or another large and established name.

5. Assassin

Really? Do you kill things for a living? I know that you are trying to make yourself sound like a badass, but I want someone who is going to help me with my business challenges, not try to impress me like a 13-year-old playing Xbox.

6. Results-Oriented (Or Results-Driven)

LinkedIn puts out an annual Top 10 of the most overused words on profiles. This one is a regular on that list. It's jargon and it means absolutely nothing. Aren't we all focused on getting results in our professional lives? Here's a general rule of thumb: If it looks like it belongs on a resume, don't put it in your headline.

7. Connector

Being a LION (LinkedIn Open Networker) on LinkedIn doesn't make you a mover and shaker who is making deals happen. Whenever I see someone who is a "Connector," I wonder who they are really connecting. And that rarely speaks to how you help your network of clients, partners, and prospects.

8. Wizard

Hey, I read Harry Potter too. But I've come to grips with the fact that I'm not going to be visited by an owl anytime soon. Unless you are talking about your Friday night Dungeons & Dragons game with your friends, leave the spellcasting out of your profile.

9. Expert

I'm going out on a limb here because there are a lot of experts on LinkedIn, but here's my take: If you must tell me that you are an expert, you probably aren't. You just think you are. Don't tell me; show me in the rest of your profile that you have the chops. (By the way, there's an exception. If you've put your 10,000 hours in, then go ahead and claim your expertise.)

Write Your About Section

A long with your profile images and headline, the About section is the third of the three most important parts of the profile. (<u>see 3.6.1</u>) It's a blank canvas of 2,000 characters and there are many different approaches you can take to communicate with your reader. That open format and blank canvas can create a lot of stress. Many people simply don't know the right approach to take when writing it. And without a clearly defined process for crafting the About section, it's all too easy to create something that is unfocused, unclear, and incomplete.

This isn't helped by the fact that many people are uncomfortable writing about themselves. This is unfortunate because it's an opportunity to have your message broadcast to everyone, everywhere, all the time. It's like having an elevator speech that's on 24 hours a day. Imagine that your profile visitor is your ideal contact. The About section is your chance to speak directly to them. Basically, your goal is to mirror what you would say in the offline world. How would you speak to your reader if you met that person at a conference or cocktail reception?

The About section is your chance to speak directly to your visitor.

If you're not a writer, putting together this section can seem daunting. But a step-by-step approach will help make this a painless process. The goal is to find a balance between giving people adequate information while not overwhelming them. They didn't come to LinkedIn because they were looking for a full autobiography, but they do want to find out more about you and what you do.

Walking the line between too much and too little information is the difference between an About section that just exists and one that drives business. When looking at how to create a great About section, it helps to start by looking at what not to do first. There are three big mistakes that people make all the time. You're going to see a lot of these examples as you surf around LinkedIn.

1. Some skip the About section completely – it's nonexistent.

They are losing out on a powerful way of influencing their visitor. When this is blank, it conveys one of a few messages, and none of them are positive. It shows that the professional in the profile could be thinking: "I'm not confident enough to write about myself," "I'm too overwhelmed by other things to think about LinkedIn," or "I'm not current with trends in business (i.e. social media) so I don't want to spend time with LinkedIn." No matter the reason, these profiles miss out on a huge opportunity, and they are creating a negative impression on their visitors.

2. There are also a lot of resume imports.

These are the people who have just cut/pasted from the Objective section on their resume. It's often filled with jargon, with phrases like "detail-oriented," "results-focused," and "team player." No one speaks like a resume in the real world, and you shouldn't speak like one on your LinkedIn profile. Not only are you communicating poorly, but if someone looks at your profile, they might think you're looking for a new gig. That's fine if you are actively in a job search. But if you aren't, you want to show that you are committed to doing good work where you currently are.

3. The opposite of the blank About section is an overloaded one.

This is when someone tosses in every piece of information they have about their professional career. It's usually overwhelming, chaotic, and long. These are not good adjectives to describe your online presence. People take one quick look at a long About section and tune out. They aren't at your LinkedIn profile for your life story, so be concise. People don't read online; they scan. Because of that, you want to make the important information easily accessible.

The first step to avoiding these mistakes is to keep your overall strategy in mind. By considering your target audience, the message you want to send them, and the business goals you are currently focused on, you will have a clear direction. Using those ideas to organize your thoughts, you'll come up with a concise, tight message that will accurately communicate your brand message to your visitors.

A simple, clear structure is the secret to mastering the About section. Let's walk through a simple template that will help you organize this information in a way that will be engaging to your visitors and make them want to do business with you. We'll do this with three short paragraphs and a call-to-action (CTA). You'll want each paragraph to be two or three sentences. We're going to keep this short, sweet, and simple.

1. Tell people what you do on a day-to-day basis.

Don't use internal jargon or fall back on your job title. For example, your reader might not know what an Account Executive or Director does at your organization. You need to tell them what you do and who you help. You can't just assume that they'll know – they aren't psychic.

This could be as basic as saying, "I'm a real estate agent who specializes in working with first-time homebuyers" or "As the Director of Marketing at Company XYZ, I'm working on new ways to let our customers know about how we can help." It's a short version of your in-person introduction. If you were at a neighborhood BBQ and someone asked you what you did, what would you say? That's how you start your About section.

2. Next, tell the reader what makes you different and/or better.

You want to find a way to differentiate yourself. Usually, this is going to include an "I" statement and a "we" statement. There's probably a reason why you are good at what you do and why people like to work with you. It might be your experience, competence, skillsets, or passion. Whatever it is, share it. Then you want to connect with your larger organization. Talk about what your company brings to the table. Your company has spent thousands of dollars, maybe more, figuring out how to market themselves. It makes sense to grab a sentence or two from them.

It could be as simple as saying, "I have 20 years of experience in the field, so I know how to solve our customers' challenges easily and effortlessly." You could share your passion: "I love when I'm able to help our employees shine." And think of the one or two sentences that you would use in describing the best parts of your company. That's what you would add here.

3. Finally, you want to share something about yourself.

People want to connect with other people online, not companies or brands. Be human. It's being profersonal™ and recognizing that your personal and professional spheres are intertwined online. Find something you feel comfortable sharing about yourself. It's not an online dating profile, so you don't have to say you like long walks on the beach, fine dining, and that you're a Virgo. Rather, share one nonprofessional activity and one detail about it.

For example, don't say that you "like to spend time with your kids" because that just shows that you are a normal human being. However, if you said that you liked to spend time with your kids and you coach their Little League team, that's more informative. If you like to bake, tell your reader about your most popular creation. If you are a live music fan, share your favorite concert experience. If you are a golfer, let people know what course you are dreaming of playing. You are looking to share a "hook" that creates a natural starting point for a conversation.

Finally, you want to add a call-to-action at the end of your About section. This is usually one sentence that invites the reader to continue the process of engaging with you. If you are looking for clients, partners, or employees, you can write something as simple as, "If you would like to talk about (insert what you do), please send me a message here on LinkedIn." Or if you want to connect with peers who are also working in the same area, you can suggest they send you a LinkedIn connection invite. The goal is to open the door for further interaction. They've come to your profile; how can you keep the conversation going?

You can still do this easily and quickly, even if you aren't a professional writer. Take a piece of paper and divide it into three sections, one for each part of the About section. For each of the steps, write down three or four ideas. Just do a quick information dump onto the paper. Then, in each section, write one sentence that tries to encapsulate everything. You'll find that you will need an extra sentence or two to fully explain what you mean. And before you know it, you'll have an About section. If you want some feedback or to be sure that you are being clear, show it to a colleague or friend whom you trust.

Sit down today and write out your About section. Experiment! It doesn't have to be perfect the first time around. You are always evolving and growing in your career. This summary of your professional life will evolve and grow with you.

3.7

Share Your Story and Not Your Resume

How do you talk about your past on LinkedIn? It's easy to look at the Experience and Education sections on your LinkedIn profile as the "resume" part of the profile. There's a slight problem, though. No one wants to read your resume. Even corporate recruiters and headhunters don't like reading them. But then how are you supposed to talk about your past work life?

Much of the confusion stems from the fact that the LinkedIn profile *did* start as a kind of online resume. In its early days, LinkedIn was a way for professionals in Silicon Valley to keep track of each other. It was an environment where short-term stints were the norm and paper resumes and contact lists were quickly out-of-date. It was a short hop from using it as a contact database to using it as a forum where people could be found for work. It stayed that way for the first year or two, and so it was natural for the first non-Silicon Valley users to upload their resumes as well when they first created their account.

Even though the platform has changed and evolved since then, most professionals still think of LinkedIn primarily as a job-finding tool. And it makes sense to add your resume to a job-finding tool, doesn't it?

But that doesn't tell the complete story. These days, to think of your LinkedIn profile as just an online resume is to think of YouTube as just online television. It completely misses that there are a wide range of new activities and interactions that it enables. In the past, you would only use a resume when you were looking for a new job. Now someone can look at your profile whenever they need to engage with you. That could be when they are thinking of hiring you, hiring your company as a vendor, or even just partnering with you on an internal company project.

This is why it's important to craft a professional story that moves beyond just a bullet-point list of your previous job responsibilities. The Experience section provides a place to share the narrative of your career arc. You don't list your past jobs just to fill in the blanks, but to show how you got to where you are today. Your past experiences are what support everything else that you are saying in your profile, from your headline to your About section.

> *It's important to craft a professional story that moves beyond just a bullet-point list of your previous job responsibilities.*

If all you do is import your resume, you've lost out. They are usually dry, convoluted collections of facts and figures couched in "resume-speak," a language that isn't used in everyday life. When was the last time you used "results-oriented" or "task-focused" when talking to your friends? Nobody wants to read that on your profile.

When outlining your experience, use language and a structure that will encourage people to read it. (see 3.7.1) Your current position section will have some similarities to your About section, obviously, because it's what you are doing in the present. There's also an opportunity to talk more in-depth about your role on a day-to-day basis and about the company that you work for. Don't assume that someone can look at your job title and know what your responsibilities are. At the same time, though, don't go overboard. People aren't at your LinkedIn profile because they couldn't find your autobiography on Amazon. They want the basics. Writing two to four sentences is enough for your current position.

Avoid glossing over your past positions. The jobs you held in the past are how you got the experience that you use today. In fact, that's how you should structure what you say here. Write a sentence about what you did at a past job. Then spend a few sentences telling your reader what you learned there that makes you awesome in your current role. Keep it simple and focus on transferable skills and experiences. And no bullet points! You don't speak in bullet points and you shouldn't write in bullet points here either.

It can sometimes be challenging to figure out if you should include certain past jobs, especially if you've been in different industries or if you've had a long career. My suggestion is to include anything that is relevant to your current role. If you've been in your industry for 20 years, your college summer job delivering newspapers doesn't need to be there unless you are now an editor or writer at a major publication. Ask yourself, "Does sharing this job help my audience understand why I'm good at what I do? Does it not connect to my overall story?"

Filling in the Education section is straightforward, but there are a few things to point out. (see 3.7.2) First off, be sure you use the right dates, which also goes for your Position entries. Include your graduate work and add your high school, especially if you are in the same area that you grew up in. You never know when someone is a fellow alum. Include all your major academic endeavors. For ongoing professional development, licenses, and other training, use the Certifications section.

The goal of your Experience and Education sections is to give a fuller picture of your professional narrative. It fills in the details to what you've outlined in your headline and your About section. Every professional has a story to share, so share your story!

3.8

Leverage Skills and Endorsements

The Skills and Expertise section (see 3.8.1) on LinkedIn caused a lot of consternation when it was introduced. Now it's largely forgotten and because of that, underused. When LinkedIn moved the keyword bank from the "Specialties" area in the Summary to its own section back in the day, it was trying to provide some structure to the process of adding keywords to the profile. At the same time, though, they started allowing users to give each other "Endorsements" on their listed Skills (and even unlisted ones). That confused the issue a bit. Were they helpful or not? Did they lead towards a valid representation of someone's abilities or were people "gaming" the system? What if someone endorsed you for a skill you didn't really have? How do you get your network to plug the right skills? The questions kept coming.

Part of the confusion stems from the fact that, at its core, the Skills and Endorsements section was designed for LinkedIn's benefit. It was a section where they could gather data about what skills people had. And even better, the Endorsements allowed for users to get third parties (other users) to, well, endorse them. This is valuable for LinkedIn because it allows them to make better recommendations for and to the recruiters on the platform. And in doing so they made it easier for recruiters to find the right talent (and recruiters are still one of the main revenue sources for LinkedIn).

As a side benefit for the rest of us, though, we now have a tool that allows us to give our profile readers more information about us. From a networking and relationship-building perspective, Skills and their endorsement by others are invaluable because they provide another level of credibility to your LinkedIn profile. It used to be that you could put anything in the Skills and Expertise section and there was no external "check" on what you added. I could have said I was an expert in skydiving even though I'm terrified of heights.

> *Skills and their endorsement by others are invaluable because they provide another level of credibility to your LinkedIn profile.*

Now you can still add any skill you want, but if no one endorses you for that skill it won't matter because it won't be as relevant or credible. If you put "Being Awesome" as a skill, but no one endorses you for it, it won't have a big impact. Conversely, if you are looking at a profile that has "Marketing" as a skill and it has 50 endorsements next to it, there's a much better chance that the person does know something about marketing. If there are 99+ endorsements, then there's a good chance they are an expert. So now there's more granularity when describing the skills we leverage in our professional lives.

Here are the steps to take to maximize your Skills and Endorsements section:

1. Check to see that you are in a profession that allows endorsements.

If you are in a field that has compliance requirements (financial or legal, for example) you might not be able to use endorsements and you should hide them. Most other professions can and should use them.

2. Add at least 25 relevant entries to the Skills section and pin the top three.

Use up to the maximum of 50 if you can. This will encourage people to endorse you for skills that you think are your strengths. If you aren't sure which ones to use, look at colleagues and peers that you respect, and see what they have used. This is a keyword bank for search terms, so include any words that describe your position or the work you do. And then pick the three most important keywords to pin to the top. By default, the profile will show the ones with the most endorsements, but you can change these to any three that you want. (see 3.8.2)

3. Endorse the people in your network.

You don't have to endorse everyone for every skill they've listed. But if someone is good at something, say so. This will encourage them to endorse you back and makes everyone's LinkedIn profiles more accurate. And it's a positive way to engage with your network!

3.9

Connect Through Community Involvement

Many professionals want to walk the line between sharing too much and too little of themselves through their social media presence. It can be challenging to find the perfect balance point between staying professional and giving your visitors a deeper glimpse of who you are personally. The goal is to share enough so that they will be comfortable starting an online dialog. And in doing so the chances are much higher you'll be able to start an offline conversation eventually.

On LinkedIn, an easy way to get started with sharing what's important to you is through the Volunteer Experience & Causes section. (see 3.9.1) Sharing your involvement in nonprofit organizations is a simple and profound way to share a broader picture of yourself online. It gives a more complete picture, which is important when sharing your brand. It allows you to be more authentic and transparent because your brand encompasses what you do professionally as well as who you are as a person.

> *Sharing your involvement in nonprofit organizations is a simple and profound way to share a broader picture of yourself online.*

People feel most comfortable doing business with people who share a background and commonalities with them. It's easier for them to build trust in someone whom they can relate to. As you look to build your connections, you can accelerate the relationship-building process by allowing your prospects to find common ground with you.

You don't have to join a group or organization just to put it on your LinkedIn profile. Like many professionals, you are probably already involved in community organizations that support causes that are important to you. It's just a matter of including that in your profile. LinkedIn makes it easy with the dedicated Volunteer Experience & Causes section. You can use it to include both current activities and past involvement. You can even list your specific roles in organizations, which is a great way to highlight the leadership positions you have held.

Is it possible to push away potential contacts by sharing what groups you support? It's possible, but it's unlikely that you will lose connections who share the same values by sharing what's important to you. But if you are concerned that a political or religious group might bring up some questions, it is OK to leave it off. Focus instead on organizations and areas that have widespread support. No one is going to be upset if you support the local animal shelter or children's hospital.

Your contacts today are savvier and more informed than they have ever been. Offer them more ways that they can engage with you on a personal level. Give them the information that allows them to feel comfortable with you and start building relationships that last a lifetime.

3.10

Keeping Up with New Profile Features

The biggest challenge in writing books about LinkedIn, or any other social media platform, is the rate at which they change and evolve. There's a reason I've put out three editions of this book in seven years: LinkedIn keeps changing! There are two types of changes that we have to manage. The first is the change in how we use the platform. The larger business context is continuously evolving, and that has an impact on the etiquette and strategies on LinkedIn. The easiest place to see that is the rush of activity that happened in response to social distancing. In 2020, there was a lot more activity on LinkedIn, but it wasn't necessarily educated activity. That's why there was a lot more "spamming" and activity that wasn't conducive to building relationships.

The other type of change is driven by LinkedIn itself. There are constant tweaks and changes to the platform. There are new features added regularly. And existing features go through revisions or are even dropped completely. The LinkedIn profile of 2021 looks vastly different from the profile of 2018, which looks completely different from the profile of 2014. The profile has been refined and added to, and there are many more ways to add content right into your profile.

Do you need to use all these additional options to have a fully optimized profile? I'm going to suggest that the answer is no. The main sections that we cover here in Section 3 are important: the images, the headline, the About section, and the Experience section. Those are critical, and with the addition of a great list of Skills and Endorsements and your community involvement, you are set.

You are in optional territory beyond those sections. The question to ask before using the additional sections is, "Will this help me tell my story to my profile visitor?" If the answer is yes, by all means, include the section. If the answer is no, feel free to skip it. Other sections include Certifications, Publications, and industry-specific information. If it's pertinent, you can add them to your profile. For example, if you write articles or online ebooks, include them in the Publications section (I certainly have). Or if you are in an industry with a lot of certification options, like financial services or computer programming, add those in. But don't feel that you need them to be successful.

And that goes for all the additional features that exist in the profile now or that will be added after this book goes to print. Whether it's adding an audio clip for name pronunciation or including your sales awards, add it if it works for you. But understand that there aren't any "secret" sections that you need. The profile will continue to evolve. There will be new sections and features that allow you to share information.

At its heart, the profile needs to provide your visitor with the information and insights necessary to understand your expertise. You want to encourage them to opt-in. Whatever helps you do that, put it in. And if it doesn't, leave it out.

3.11

Profile Advice for Younger Professionals

There's a circular trap that hits most young people when they enter the job market. They run into the challenge of trying to get experience when they don't have any. They end up asking themselves, "How can I get the experience I need to be qualified for this job when no one will hire me because I don't have experience?"

If you are a recent college grad or have recently been a college grad, you'll know that there's a 21st-century twist to the problem. It goes something like this:

> "I am new to the workforce and everyone says that my generation is totally social media savvy. So I should have a killer LinkedIn profile to help me get work. But what do I put on my "professional record of note" when my professional record consists of two internships and waiting tables during the summer at my local pizza place? How do I get something to put on my profile when I can't get a job because there's nothing on my profile?!"

First, if you're in that situation, breathe in and breathe out. It's going to be OK. We've all been there. Secondly, understand that LinkedIn is great precisely because you can use it to show what experience you do have even though you might not have a long work history. It's a great way to tell your story and frame the way potential employers will view you.

When companies hire, they are looking for someone who can do the job. That might sound obvious but think about what that means. The interviewer is looking for someone who has a high likelihood of success in the new position. That's why experience is important. It's a good indicator of whether you will be able to handle the responsibilities of the role. But you can use LinkedIn to fill in the hole left by your lack of experience. It can illustrate that you have the skills necessary to do the job even if you don't have a long line of previous experience.

> *Your LinkedIn Profile can illustrate that you have the skills necessary to do the job even if you don't have a long line of previous experience.*

Here are five places on your LinkedIn profile where you can look like a competent professional instead of a green rookie:

1. Update your headshot.

Do you still have a photo cropped from that fraternity social (the last time you were dressed up)? It might be time to get a new one. The trick here is not to look older than you are. The trick is to look polished and competent. Are you someone whom an employer would want to represent them? Look around your area for networking events that have a photographer giving free social media headshots. And while you're there, do some networking.

2. Use the right headline.

If it says "Student at XYZ University," time to change it. That doesn't tell a potential employer anything about you. Your LinkedIn profile headline is just like a newspaper article headline. It should create interest and excitement for the visitor. They should know right from the start what you are about. Try this: *Professional in (your field or industry) focused on (the specific area you want to work in).*

3. Write a compelling About section.

This is huge because this is where you can create the context for your visitors. You can influence how potential employers see you. Imagine that someone is hiring for a job you'd love and would be great at. They are sitting across the table from you and they've just asked, "Why should I pick you? What will you bring to the team?" Use this summary to share that answer!

4. Frame your experience.

You might not have a long list of experiences, but make sure that the work experience you have adequately shows what you can do. But don't make this a bullet-pointed resume section. Tell your reader about the learning opportunities you had in each position. What abilities did you develop at each role that you can transfer to your next position?

5. Add your volunteer work.

More and more young people participate in volunteer activities. And even if you aren't getting paid, it still counts as experience. Helping to organize a fundraiser or leading a community clean-up day are experiences that translate directly into the for-profit world. Use the volunteer section to not only show your involvement in areas that concern you, but also how you've refined your skillsets.

By the way, if all of these profile sections don't help you tell your story, then your LinkedIn Profile is providing you with another service: It's showing you where you have gaps in your professional experience. Look for ways to fill those gaps, possibly through internships, apprenticeships, or even an entrepreneurial effort.

When you use these tools, you can create a killer LinkedIn profile, no matter that you are at the start of your career. You'll give yourself the best opportunity to move past the no job/no experience dichotomy.

Section 4

FIND AND ENGAGE YOUR NETWORK

A robust LinkedIn profile is an important foundation, but it's just a start. Once you've established your brand online, you can look to engage more fully with your network. To use LinkedIn as a social networking tool, though, you need to have a network! You can start by bringing your existing connections into LinkedIn. From there you can use it as a channel to create new connections to move beyond your current relationships. No matter what your career goals are, you can align your networking activities with what you want to accomplish.

Each of us will bring a different set of goals and expectations to LinkedIn. Let's look at who should be in your network, the etiquette of how to engage with them, and even how big your network should be. This is where you start moving past the passive uses of LinkedIn and start engaging with the 700+ million members on the platform.

What Is Your LinkedIn Network?

Before digital technology, it was relatively easy to define our network. It consisted of the people we had met over the course of our life and career. It was made up of those whom we had physically encountered or maybe a pen pal or two. Our networking focused on those we had engaged with based on where we lived, went to school, and worked.

But if you had to describe your LinkedIn network, how would you define it? Our online network still contains the people with whom we've had direct contact over the years. But there are so many more opportunities these days. Now we can connect with others around the country and the world with a click of a button. We can reach out to thought leaders in our field, possible partners or clients, and fellow industry practitioners without ever meeting them in the offline world.

Not only can we create that initial connection, but our newsfeed keeps us up to date on the activity within our network with minimal effort. A few minutes on our computer or phone can let us know a lot about what is happening with our contacts. Spending just a little time to scroll through the newsfeed keeps us informed with what's happening in our field and the business world at large. Now we have a way to find out the needs and opportunities of a much larger cross-section of our potential partners and customers. We don't have to network exclusively with the small group of professionals that we run into during our daily business lives.

And we can connect with a much larger group of people by leveraging technology. This expanded network has a lot of practical benefits. Researcher Mark Granovetter illuminated the power of what he called "weak connections" in his ground-breaking paper "The Strength of Weak Ties." These were people with whom we had contact less than once a week but more than once a year. We had some relationship with them, but it wasn't a close connection. And what Grannoveter found was that these weak connections were more likely to lead to job opportunities, possible partnerships, and prospective clients precisely because we don't see them very often. They spent their time in different spheres of influence, exposed to completely different people and information. And by running into them every once in a while, we gained access and entry into those different spheres of influence. That's where the real power of your networking relationships came in.

When you look at many of your LinkedIn connections, that's what you will find: Almost all of them are weak connections. And that's a good thing! LinkedIn has given us a platform that we can use to stay in touch with a much broader group of our weak connections with little extra energy and time. That means that your LinkedIn network is much more than a collection of names and resume information. It's an environment, a matrix of relationships, that we cultivate for business success. As you build your network on LinkedIn, you're creating the potential for good things to happen. You're building access and reach for future opportunities. Your LinkedIn network becomes a valuable resource that follows you for your entire career, from job to job. It's there for introductions, leads, feedback, support, and camaraderie.

LinkedIn has given us a platform that we can use to stay in touch with a much broader group of our weak connections with little extra energy and time.

So your LinkedIn network is much more than just a list of connections and some information about them. It's much more than just a professional Rolodex. Or rather, it can be much more if you put the time and attention on it to build those relationships. The goal isn't to become best buddies with everyone in your network. Mark Grannoveter showed that you didn't need to do that to have your network be a resource for you. Rather, you want to use LinkedIn to create a forum where we can connect with people whom we can help succeed and who can help us succeed.

4.2

Who to Connect With

Social media platforms have broken down the geographic barriers that limited our networks in the past. Now, physical proximity doesn't hold us back from connecting. We can reach across the world to engage with others just as easily as we can connect with a coworker down the hall. But that freedom doesn't necessarily help us when we're deciding who we should connect with. So the most basic question when building your LinkedIn network is: "Who should I connect with?"

Let's start with an important caveat. Your LinkedIn network, the connections you have, and the relationships you have with them is yours. You are the final arbiter of who should and shouldn't be in your network. There aren't any hard and fast rules in building your network that apply to everyone, so it's important that you are comfortable with whom you connect with and how you engage with them. Don't feel that you must engage in an online strategy just because someone suggested it (even me).

With that out of the way, we can look at who you bring into your network. Should you just connect with everyone? Probably not. Just because online networking allows us to connect with everyone doesn't mean that we should. There are some professionals on LinkedIn who call themselves LIONs (LinkedIn Open Networkers), and their goal is to build as many connections as possible. They want to hit the LinkedIn cap of 30,000 connections. While there's nothing inherently wrong with this, you don't want to confuse reach with access. Thinking that you can have a tight network of tens of thousands is like thinking that everybody in the phone book is your friend just because you have access to their phone number.

The goal is to balance reach and access. The place to start is with the people with whom you interact in the offline world. Start by making sure that you connect with colleagues, customers, and partners in your current role. Even if you engage with them every day right now, in five years it's possible that some will have moved on and it will be good to have that online connection. In the same way, reach out to the people you knew at past positions, schools, and organizations. LinkedIn will give you a great tool to stay in touch with those people.

> *The goal of building an effective LinkedIn network is to balance reach and access.*

The next group of connections to add consists of those people you run into during your regular business activities. When you meet someone at a conference, a networking event, or another professional event, it's a good idea to follow up with a LinkedIn invite in the subsequent days. You don't have to see a direct and obvious business goal. Simply add a short note to the invite that says, "It was great meeting you at _____. I'd like to stay connected and see if there's a way to help each other in the future."

Just adding those connections to your LinkedIn network will help it grow over time. But you don't have to stop there. You can extend your offline networking activities into the online world. When one of your first-level connections shares content from one of their first-level connections, you can engage with that content and start a conversation. It can be useful to reach out to that person who is a second-level connection to see if they'd like to connect.

And along those lines, there's nothing wrong with reaching out to aspirational connections. These are people whom you haven't met in the offline world but would like to. They might be leaders in your field, community, or favorite organization. Or they might be someone who runs in the same circles as you but whom you haven't met yet. You can send an invite that says, "We haven't had a chance to meet yet, but I've seen your (postings, books, online content). I'd love to connect on LinkedIn. Let me know if I can help with anything." Maybe they will connect, and maybe not, but it doesn't hurt to ask.

And that brings up the question of which LinkedIn invitations you should accept. As I pointed out at the beginning of the section, your LinkedIn network is yours and you are the final arbiter of who you let in. My friend Andy Crestodina, who is a prominent marketing expert and speaker, has a simple decision-making process that you can learn from. If someone invites him to connect, and they share either an industry (marketing) or location (Chicago) that's relevant to him, then he'll accept it. If they don't share at least one of those two groups, he probably won't.

Of course, be aware that there are spambots and charlatans on LinkedIn just like there are in every corner of the internet. So if someone you don't know reaches out but their profile looks fake or just "off," it's totally OK to skip over the invite. When you look at a profile and the individual is from another country and the profile is incomplete or doesn't make a lot of sense, it's best to decline. And always remember that you can choose to disconnect from any of your connections whenever you want to. That means if you want to change your mind, you can.

There are a lot of different ways to construct your LinkedIn network, but it's more useful to be inclusive than exclusive. So reach out and start connecting!

4.3

Connect with People You Don't Know

People often think that the power of your LinkedIn network is in your direct connections. That's not exactly correct. That's because one of the most valuable assets on LinkedIn isn't the people you know. It's the people that *they* know.

By providing access to these second- and third-level connections, LinkedIn provides you an amazing resource that you can use to gain new clients, new vendors, and new partners. These connections used to be "hidden." You wouldn't normally sit down at someone's desk and flip through their Rolodex. Now, that's exactly what you can do. You can find the exact people you want to meet, find out information about them, and see how you are connected to them. Even the Search function allows you to organize the results by relationship. (see 4.3.1) You can see which LinkedIn users are in your network easily and quickly. For example, if you wanted to find all the CPAs in your network who are your second-level connections, it's only a few clicks away.

Once you've found a professional you'd like to meet in your larger network, you have a few options. It can be as simple as sending a message to your shared first-level contact through LinkedIn. Or you can even send them a quick email or give them a quick call. There's nothing wrong with finding the information on LinkedIn and then moving to another platform!

When you do ask a fellow connection to introduce you to someone that they're connected to, there are a few things to keep in mind. Keep your introduction "asks" short and sweet. Be straightforward and ask for what you want, and always give an out. It could be something like this:

> "Hi Bill,
>
> Would you mind introducing me to your contact Sue Smith? She works at Company XYZ and I'm looking to work with them. I was hoping she might be able to help me with some insights into their marketing needs. If you don't have a strong relationship with her and don't feel comfortable passing on the introduction, that's totally OK. Thanks!"

Another option would be to reach out to new connections directly on LinkedIn. When looking at the profile of someone who is your second- or third-level connection, you will see the intermediary connections that you both share. But remember, just because you have a shared connection, they might not know that common connection that well. So be careful when you are name-dropping. To reach out to someone on LinkedIn whom you don't know, simply craft a customized invite to that person that references your shared connection. Again, simple is best:

"Hi Lisa,

I found your profile on LinkedIn and saw that we both know Jim Smith at Company XYZ. I've known him since we both worked at Acme Inc. These days I'm also a project manager in the technology field and would love to connect with a fellow colleague. Have a great day!"

Or maybe you don't have a shared connection. That doesn't mean that you can't invite them to your network. In this scenario, it's important to establish a reason why you are reaching out. It improves the likelihood that they'll accept the invitation, and it also gives them some context for the relationship. They'll know why it can be useful for them to connect with you:

"Hi Jamie,

I wanted to reach out because {we met at X event; I saw that you were at Company Y and we've worked with them; I saw your post about Z; I love connecting with fellow Northwestern Wildcats.} I'd love to connect. I do a lot of work in the _____ space, and if I can ever be of assistance, let me know."

By using these guidelines for reaching out to new connections on LinkedIn beyond your existing relationships, you'll create a network that has even more opportunities. Not all of these connections will have an immediate "payoff." That's OK! By building the relationship and creating some social capital before you have a direct need, you'll create some networking karma for the future.

Engage Your Alumni Network on LinkedIn

O f all the networks we build in our lives, one of the earliest and deepest networks we create is that of our alma maters. People take their connection to their school seriously. The fundraising department at your school depends on it when they have students call and ask you for money. Take me for example. I'm a busy guy and I don't have a lot of spare time just lying around. But if you want to have five minutes of my time, call me and tell me when you graduated from Northwestern University. I'll give you a few minutes.

In the past, if you wanted to network with your fellow alums you had to wait for your next reunion to roll around. Or if you were lucky, the alumni association would have events in your area where you could meet others from your school. That would only work, though, if you stayed around your school after graduation or were in a major metropolitan area.

LinkedIn has done a lot to beef up its alumni section. Because LinkedIn has 700+ million members who have self-identified themselves, your classmates are already there. They've already filled in the "Education" box with their school so you don't have to go searching them out. Whether you are a recent graduate or a graduate of the class of (mumble, mumble, mumble), it's a great tool to use when you are looking to expand your network.

At the heart of the alumni section is a powerful search engine that allows you to find your fellow alumni. (see 4.4.1) You can filter the results by where alumni live, what industry or companies they work in, and even what they studied while in school. The date filter allows you to find alums who went to school during a specific period. This is a great way to find your fellow classmates. And you can also sort through them by the degree of connection on LinkedIn. For example, there are over 3,000 members on LinkedIn who were Northwestern Wildcats during the same years I was in school and who are also second-level connections. That makes sense, because I'm sure that my roommates, friends, and classmates knew a lot of people I didn't. If I wanted to reach out to those people, I could leverage my school connection and we also know someone in common. That makes it a lot easier to start a conversation with them!

There are many ways you could leverage the alumni section. For example, those 3,000+ second-level connections that I went to school with have spread around the country and the world and into almost every conceivable industry and job. If I was looking to move, to work for a new organization, or even to change career paths, I could reach out to my connections in those areas so I could ask questions and get some feedback. If I was interested in making inroads into a company because I wanted to get a job there or because I was in sales and they were a great prospect, I would absolutely start with fellow alumni. When you are prospecting for new opportunities, the hardest thing to do is get someone to pick up the phone and talk to you. You wouldn't expect someone to buy from you or hire you just because you went to the same school together, but it can be the proverbial "foot in the door" that helps you start the conversation.

Beyond the search feature, your school's homepage also includes a newsfeed where alumni can communicate with each other, a listing of notable alumni, and links to your school's LinkedIn Groups. How you use all this information is up to you, but it's a great resource as you build your career!

Go 'Cats!

Pay Attention to the Signals in Your LinkedIn Newsfeed

B ecoming a great networker is about much more than talking. It's also critical to listen to your contacts and understand their needs. People will tell you what's important to them, what challenges they are having, and how they can help you. But only if you are paying attention. Social media hasn't changed the need to listen, but it has changed where you do your "listening."

A lot of the focus on LinkedIn centers on how to share content. What gets overlooked is your ability to hone in on the information your network is sharing with you. The LinkedIn newsfeed is a fantastic aggregator of everything that is going on in your network. A few minutes a day can keep you in the know and cue you into important happenings in the professional lives of your colleagues, prospects, clients, peers, and partners. That's what is exciting about using LinkedIn for listening: The ability to leverage your time and find lots of information quickly and easily.

> *The LinkedIn newsfeed is a fantastic aggregator of everything that is going on in your network.*

As your network grows into the hundreds and even thousands on LinkedIn, it can be a little overwhelming to sift through all of this information. There are filters that allow you to switch between seeing the most recent activity from your network and the "top" activity that has the most engagement. They are accessed through the upper right hand of the Newsfeed. (see 4.5.1) Usually, it's best to see the top posts. The LinkedIn algorithm works behind the scenes to share content that it thinks you will find relevant. Every once in a while, you can switch to see all of the most recent activity and you'll get a more complete overview. It's a little overwhelming, but you can skim through to see if there's a connection that the algorithm is overlooking.

There's more information on the LinkedIn algorithm in Section 5 and how it determines whose content you see (and who sees your content). In the meantime, it's important to realize that your LinkedIn newsfeed is an important source of business intelligence. Your connections are sharing information that they think is important. While you are reading through the newsfeed, you can look for information that signals an area where you can help. These are "triggers," where a connection is sharing that they have a challenge that you could help solve. You might be able to help because you have insights into the problem they are facing, or you might be able to introduce them to a potential employee or partner. Or maybe your company provides the service they need.

The triggers will sometimes be direct and sometimes you'll have to read between the lines as well. But keeping your eyes open to the signals that your connections are sharing is a key step to leveraging your online network. This makes LinkedIn a great resource to find out about potential clients or jobs, industry events and conferences, and the latest trends and news in your field.

4.6

Engaging with Your Connections' Content

When looking at how to actually "do" things on LinkedIn, the first activity that pops to mind for most users is posting content to share with their network. That's certainly a powerful place to start. But considering that less than 1% of LinkedIn users share content, it's likely that you aren't posting a lot to LinkedIn. And while you'll find some easy ways to do that in Section 5, there's an easier place to start engaging. Instead of looking at how you can "talk" on LinkedIn, you can learn how to "listen actively."

When looking at LinkedIn engagement in general, there are three ways to take action when you interact with other members. They are the 3 "Cs": you should *Concentrate*, *Curate*, and then *Create*. *Concentrate* means to focus on the content that your connections are sharing. You put your attention on them. *Curate* means to gather content from other sources (for example, other websites, blogs, or thought-leaders) and share it by posting to LinkedIn. You give full attribution, of course, but you can also add your own insights and perspectives on the information. Finally, you have *Creation*. That's where you are creating your own posts, whether that means a text-only post, a video, an image, or one of the other options we'll explore in Section 5.

The three Cs work in concert with each other, and a good LinkedIn strategy involves all three. That being said, *Concentration* should be the foundation of your LinkedIn engagement. If you envision them as a pyramid or ladder, *Concentration* is at the base with *Curation* and *Creation* are built upon it. Because while you might only post content a few times a week, you can and should be engaging with your network regularly – daily if possible. To use an offline metaphor, you have one mouth and two ears in that proportion because you should be listening twice as much as you are speaking. Well, online, you should be reading through the posts of your network and responding appropriately much more than you are sharing your own content.

There is quite a lot of information that you can glean by scrolling through your LinkedIn newsfeed. (see 4.6.1) Everything that is there has been posted by someone in your network because they think it's important. That means that there are professional insights that you can discover as well as what is happening with your networking partners on a personal level. Whether it's a promotion, a job change, an industry analysis, or an event announcement, you can find out a lot just by surfing through your newsfeed regularly.

You take it up a notch when you engage with the content your connections are sharing. You can **Like**, **Comment**, **Share**, and **Send** in response to any of the posts on your feed. And by taking the time to do so, you can create conversations and interactions that will help in the online world as well as have an offline impact. You are building relationships and creating credibility that you can leverage in the near and short term.

You take your online networking up a notch when you engage with the content your connections are sharing.

When you **Like** a post on your newsfeed, the original poster gets a notification. This is a quick and easy way to show up on their radar. It's a relatively superficial interaction, so you don't want to rely on likes for all of your engagement. But because they are fast and easy, they are useful when you just have a few minutes to scroll through your newsfeed or when you just want to give a quick bit of validation. You can also use the different icons, such as ones indicating that you want to celebrate, support, or love, the post. But their impact is the same.

The **Comment** feature is powerful because it allows you to start a conversation with the person who posted the content, or even with other commenters. This is a great way to engage with your contacts and show that you are paying attention. You can ask a question, share an example, or even pull in another connection to have them contribute. Also, there are usually way more Likes than Comments, so you can stand out much more by commenting. The downside is that they do take time and focus to do well. You can't just zoom through a lot of comments. So these are best when you have a minute or two to add something useful to the online conversation.

By **Sharing** a post, you take a post on your newsfeed and share it "whole cloth" with your network. You also have the opportunity to add text as an introduction (more on that in Section 5). This is a great way to validate the original poster of the content. You're basically saying, "I thought this was so important, I'm going to share it with everyone I'm connected to." The only challenge is that Shares don't have as much reach as an original post. So only use it occasionally when you want to give a strong show of support.

Finally, the **Send** feature allows you to send a post directly to a connection. This is the 21st-century version of clipping a newspaper article and mailing it to someone. By Sending a post to someone, you can highlight an important topic, inform them of an industry event, or let them know you are thinking of them when you aren't together. It's a great way to share information and reinforce the bond between the two of you.

As you can see, there are a lot of ways that you can concentrate on your network connections. By engaging with the content they share, you reinforce the relationships you are developing in your network. It helps on the human-to-human level because you are building social capital. It also has an effect on the LinkedIn algorithm, so you'll see more of their content in your newsfeed, and vice versa. It's a great way of staying top-of-mind and relevant even if you aren't seeing a connection that frequently in the offline world.

4.7

The Hidden Value of "Liking" Job Anniversaries

Over the years, one of the most consistently maligned features on LinkedIn has been the job anniversary notification. Over and over I hear some form of, "Why is LinkedIn gumming up my feed? Why should I care if Bill Jones has been at Company XYZ for 6 years? Does 'liking' that really mean anything?"

Well, yes it does.

To explain the value of liking job anniversaries (or similar updates like birthdays or promotions), we have to look at something else that people don't really enjoy: small talk. It's easy to bash small talk. We think that it's an awkward and superficial conversation with people we don't know well. It's something we try to avoid. But that's not the whole story on small talk. There are some powerful effects that we need to be aware of.

When linguistic experts look at how people interact with each other, they often look at something called *phatic communication.* It's defined as verbal or nonverbal communication that has a social function as opposed to a content function. It's communication that's not meant to convey information, but rather to show that the lines of communication are open. It reinforces the social bond between two people.

Examples of phatic communication include waving hello, smiling, or saying "How are you?" when you first greet someone. The content of the question "How are you?" would indicate that you are looking for the other person to describe their mental and physical state. But really, you are just saying that you are ready to engage in a conversation with that person. You're saying that you are ready and willing to connect.

Much of the interaction on social media is relatively shallow. But just because there isn't a lot of depth in every post doesn't mean that those posts aren't meaningful. A lot of them have a social function separate from their actual content. "Liking" a job anniversary on LinkedIn is just one example of how this phatic communication can play out online. Even liking or commenting on a post has a phatic effect. You're showing that you are engaged in the relationship and that the lines of communication are open. The other person might not take you up on it right then, but they know it's available.

It's like waving to a friend when they come into the conference room for a meeting. They might not start a conversation with you right away, but they know they can later. Imagine what would happen if they walked in the room and you ignored them. That would close off the possibility of interaction.

The birthday reminders that pop on LinkedIn have a similar effect. Even if you aren't best friends with someone, or even that close, a birthday greeting sends out positive karma. It might not lead to a conversation immediately, but it will allow your next interaction to go a little more smoothly. Even just a short note of a sentence or two can be a good idea (try not to use the stale recommended templates).

So even if acknowledging a job anniversary doesn't lead to a conversation right then and there, you're now poised to have a better conversation down the line.

4.8

Leverage LinkedIn Groups

inkedIn Groups are one of the easiest ways to *do* something on LinkedIn. And they are a great place to start your online networking. Used correctly, Groups make the huge 700+ million online networking event that is LinkedIn much more manageable, and they allow you to leverage your social media time and effort efficiently. But because there are so many groups, it's important that you align your approach to LinkedIn Groups to your larger business goals. It's a slippery path and you could easily spend hours and hours connecting in LinkedIn Groups with little to show for it.

LinkedIn has struggled to make Groups a go-to destination like Facebook has, but there are still a lot of great conversations happening in them. Because they cluster around professional topics and industries, it's a good way to connect with people who share a common professional interest but aren't directly connected to you. Here's a simple process for finding the right Groups to join, engaging with them intelligently, and getting a good return on your time.

1. Set your expectations correctly.

LinkedIn Groups are a powerful forum, but they aren't a silver bullet that will solve all your problems. Keep in mind what you can reasonably expect from your efforts. It would be great to get a new client or job the first time you participate in a group discussion. But you should view groups as an incremental and additive tool. Just like offline relationships take time to cultivate, it will also take time to build your relationships with your colleagues in the groups you join. Keep the right expectations in mind.

2. Create a group hotlist.

You can join up to fifty groups on LinkedIn. But it would be incredibly unwieldy to participate in that many at the same time. Five to ten is usually a good number, and you will want to spread your group participation among several categories. They can be industry or trade groups. They can also be geographically based or alumni groups from schools or companies. The exact mix will be based on your goals and your existing networking. You will often be able to find ones that combine more than segment (for example, an alumni group from your alma mater comprised of people in your industry).

3. Find your groups.

With over 2 million groups, you might think that it would be easy to find ones to join. You'd be right and wrong. It's quite easy to find ones that *sound* like they are right up your alley. But finding good groups that are worth your time can be a little tougher. Here are three ways to find possibilities.

- From your connections. Look at your favorite (and most successful) connections on LinkedIn and scroll through their groups. This is a great way to find groups that pertain to your industry and geographic area. The bonus: these groups already contain someone you know.

- Use the Group Search Function. From the top search bar, use keywords to conduct a general search and then select Groups. (see 4.8.1) You'll find ones that are relevant to your areas of interest.

- Start your own. This can be a great way to fill an unmet need, but keep in mind that running a good group takes a lot of time and focus. If you aren't ready to invest that energy, go back to steps 1 and 2.

4. Choose the right groups.

It's easy to find groups that are relevant to your interests. But unfortunately, not all of them will be useful. A lot of them are ghost towns that lack discussions, are full of self-promoters, or are too big or too little. A few things to look for:

- Groups can vary from 20 members to 20,000. A good place to get started is with groups that hover around 300 to 400 members. You can add a few of the very large groups (10,000+) to get a broader reach as well.

- Open groups allow anyone to join (so they are often bigger) and tend to be a little more chaotic. Closed groups have a moderator that filters potential members, and they are often more tightly focused.

- When was the last post? If it wasn't within a week, it's likely that there is little happening in the group. Also, make sure the discussions aren't dominated by a few people spamming the group with irrelevant information.

5. Participate!

Once you've gotten a feel for the group and the flow of conversation, it's time to dive in. The easiest way to get started is by responding to what other members are posting. "Liking" a discussion can be a simple point of entry because all you need to do is click the button! But if there is a discussion that you can comment on, take the opportunity to join in. You're in this group to make connections, and you can't do that until you start connecting.

4.9

Research Your Networking Partners and Business Contacts

You did it. You got the meeting that you've been pursuing for months. It could be with a prospective client, business partner, or investor. Or maybe it's a well-connected center of influence in your industry who could introduce you to new opportunities. You've got your pitch rehearsed and you know your presentation rocks. You've got your best outfit back from the cleaners (or at least you pressed your shirt if it's on Zoom). You are ready to go.

But hang on a second. There's something else you that you should do before you go into that meeting. How much do you know about the person you are about to meet? There's a saying that most sales are won or lost before the conversation ever starts. And that applies if you are selling a product, your ideas, or yourself. The more information you have on your meeting partner, the more effective you can be. Going into a meeting blind is a rookie mistake, and one that you can avoid easily thanks to social media.

LinkedIn is a must-visit before you start your next business meeting. When you visit someone's LinkedIn profile, you access a wealth of information that will make your conversations richer and more effective. Here are three things to look for in a LinkedIn profile to take your conversation to the next level:

1. Find a connection.

Don't underestimate the power of a common background. You shouldn't manufacture a flimsy connection just to have one, but people like people who are like them. Use LinkedIn to connect the dots. Think about the last time you met a stranger who happened to go to the same school you did or was from your hometown. You want to create that same warm feeling in your conversation. Before you meet with someone, look at the schools, employers, and organizations that populate their career because you might have an overlapping experience. Even if there isn't a direct connection, you can still find similarities. Maybe you both went to a Pac-12 school, or maybe you worked in the same industry.

By the way, you don't have to be creepy when you bring up this information. It's common practice these days for people to research using LinkedIn. Simply say, "I had a chance to look at your LinkedIn profile before we met, and I noticed _____." It shows that you cared enough to look them up but lets them know you weren't stalking them online.

2. Find a question.

One of the best ways to start and deepen a conversation with someone is to get them talking about a topic they care about. Even though you are walking into a meeting with your own agenda, focusing the conversation on them in the beginning can win major points. It's like a first date. If all you do is talk about yourself, it won't go very well.

The trick here is to be genuinely interested. You can ask about their professional background, or it might be something a little more personal that comes through in their profile: "I saw that you worked at Company XYZ – what was that like?" "What made you choose to study History at University ABC?" "I saw on your LinkedIn profile that you ran the Boston Marathon. What was the hardest part of the race?"

3. Find a referral.

It's great that you got the meeting. But pros think towards the future and the next meeting. If you are fired up to talk with this person, my guess is that they know other people you would want to meet. People tend to spend time with people like themselves. Use their LinkedIn profile to see who else they are connected to and use that information to ask for a referral.

Again, you don't want to be creepy or pushy. But if you feel the conversation goes well, ask for an introduction. Make it as simple as, "I saw on LinkedIn that you know _____. How do you know her? I'd love to meet her because I think we'd be a good fit with her company. Would you feel OK about introducing us?"

Even three minutes on a LinkedIn profile can give you the information to take your next business meeting from good to great. Don't miss out!

Ask for Help on LinkedIn

Your LinkedIn network contains a full range of relationships, from your best friends and family to people you haven't even met yet in the offline world. It's important to keep that spectrum in mind when you ask for help through LinkedIn. You don't want to assume a close relationship with all your connections. At the same time, you don't need to avoid asking for help from others. It could be a college friend, a colleague from a past job, or your sister's friend. They have access to information, insights, and connections that you don't. It makes sense to leverage LinkedIn to ask your weak connections for help, but there's a right and wrong way to do it.

Since you might not know these people well, it's important to create the proper context for your ask. But the overall etiquette isn't that much different from asking for help in the offline world. The most important thing to realize is that although LinkedIn is a new communication medium, you've been communicating your whole life. So whatever approach you'd take in the real life is one you can take online. There are four pieces of the puzzle to keep in mind when reaching out for help on LinkedIn:

It's important to create the proper context for your ask.

1. Time it right.

How long should you wait before you ask for help? If you haven't seen someone in five years, and then you reconnect with them on LinkedIn, can you ask them for an introduction the next day? That's a very real scenario and the answer is: sometimes. There are no hard and fast rules to this, but keep in mind how you would act in the real world if you weren't using LinkedIn. If you ran into the person at a class reunion and would feel comfortable giving them a call the next day, then go for it. If not, spend a little time building the relationship through LinkedIn before you ask for help.

2. Give a "Because."

People love to know why something is happening. When you reach out on LinkedIn, tell them why you are doing it. It helps give some context for your request. It can be as simple as saying, "I wanted to see if you'd introduce me to the person at your company who is responsible for _____, because I would feel a lot more comfortable than if I had to cold call them."

3. Leave an out.

No one likes being trapped in a corner. You always want to leave your connection the opportunity to say "no" without feeling bad. Maybe they'd love to introduce you to their boss who's hiring, but they just came back from a staff meeting where the boss said how sick she was of interviewing people right now. When interacting with your weak connections, you don't know the backstory. Give them an out so they can refuse your request gracefully if they'd like to.

4. Express gratitude.

We're all busy, so the fact that they even read your message and considered your request is great. Let them know you appreciate their time. And let them know you appreciate their effort no matter the result. From the very first message, be very clear with your gratitude. And if they do help with an introduction or some information, take a few minutes to compose a nice thank-you note. You can even send it through LinkedIn.

When you put these steps together, it looks something like this:

"Hi Juan,

It was great connecting with your last month at the Annual Conference and I've enjoyed seeing your posts here on LinkedIn. Do you know Lisa Smith on your product marketing team well enough to introduce us? I saw that you were connected. It looks like her department is hiring and I wanted to find out more information to see if I would be a good fit. And if you don't know her well enough, no worries. Thank you so much for any help you can give."

These four steps are great for asking for help from all your contacts, whether they are someone you see every day or once a year.

But remember that much of the value of LinkedIn lies in your ability to build relationships with the people in your network on a consistent basis. One of the best ways to use it is to invest some time and attention in your network on a regular basis. When you do this, you'll find that when you need to ask for help, it's an easy and natural process.

4.11

Avoid These LinkedIn Faux Pas

Since LinkedIn has secured its place as the online extension of offline networking, it suffers a bit of "guilt by association." The same fears and hang-ups that haunt offline networking have followed us online. And when you're afraid of making mistakes or doing something wrong, it prevents you from fully engaging. But you don't have to worry about being a jerk online if you keep in mind the same etiquette rules that work offline. Here are a few of the ways that people act like jerks on LinkedIn, and the best ways to avoid them.

1. Send introduction requests with no customization.

Would you walk up to someone at a business event and have the first sentence out of your mouth be, "Here's my card. Can I have your contact info and access to your Rolodex?" Of course not! They would be justifiably wary. Remember that when you send an invite on

LinkedIn – because you are asking for access to someone's network and their attention when you ask to connect.

Write a one- to three-sentence introduction that tells the person why you'd like to connect on LinkedIn, especially if you haven't met in the offline world yet. Give them some context for your request. "I'd like to sell you something" is not going to cut it.

2. Pull a bait and switch with your introduction.

We've all met the person who is initially super-friendly and solicitous. Ninety seconds in, though, the conversation takes a twist. Suddenly they just want to sell you something. I met a mortgage broker once who asked me if I was looking to buy a house or knew anyone who was within two minutes of meeting me. I was like, "Whoa, slow down a bit." There was no relationship established and the ask was inappropriate. Would you ask somebody to marry you just two minutes after you met them?

Take the time to build a relationship and provide value before you ask the person to do something. Don't "Connect and Pitch" by trying to sell something to someone immediately. And if you feel you might be jumping the gun, say so: "I know we haven't been connected for long yet, but I wanted to let you know that..."

3. Send super-long messages

We all know the person who can't shut up and can't get to the point. I once belonged to a networking group that had a member whom I would reflexively avoid. No conversation with her would last less than ten minutes, and I never did any of the talking. It was easier to avoid her. And even though she would talk about how she could help my clients, I never once sent business to her.

Keep messages short. A lot of professionals get poor results from their InMails and other communication because they treat them like information dumps. People don't have that much time. Get right to the point: here's who I am, here's why I'm writing, here's what I'd like for you to do.

4. Post content about your product/ service and nothing else.

The people who talk too much are usually the same people who talk about themselves over and over (they need to talk about something, after all). In the end, though, others don't care to hear about the details of their product/service/life. We tune those people out. It's the same on LinkedIn. I knew a recruiter who filled my newsfeed with the minutiae of every position he was filling. He didn't stay in my newsfeed for long.

Share content that is directly related to your offering between 20 and 35% of the time. Mix it up with information that could help your target audience and a personal piece occasionally.

5. Ask for an introduction without providing an out.

If I ask you for an introduction, I'm hoping to gain credibility with the new person by extension. I'm hoping to be carried on the coattails of your relationship and borrowing a little of the credibility that you've already established. But what if we were at an event and I asked you to introduce me to someone you knew by dragging you over to them? That would put you on the spot, and I wouldn't know the context and backstory. That puts you in a very awkward position. For example, maybe you don't get along with the person I'm hoping to meet, even though you work together.

When asking for an introduction through LinkedIn, add, "If it's not a good time to introduce us, that's completely OK."

6. Hijack conversations with off-topic promotions.

You're standing at a conference cocktail reception with a few people you've just met. Everyone is having an interesting conversation about the sessions you've attended, and *bam*, a salesperson walks up, nods his head for a minute, and then tries to steer the conversation to his company's new software package. Not only is it annoying, but it ruins the vibe that you had with your other conversational partners. You don't like when others do it, so why do it to them?

Listen to the conversations before you start posting. Read all the comments on a post. And there's nothing wrong with lurking in a group to get a sense of the topics before you start contributing. It takes a little longer but it's much more effective.

7. Post inappropriate, too personal, or fluffy material.

I have yet to meet someone who hasn't heard an off-color joke or a "too much information" admission in a professional setting (there's nothing like hearing about someone's latest rash). Some people are trying to create a closer relationship, and sometimes they are just socially awkward. In any case, it's not good. In the same way, LinkedIn should be about professional topics and personal topics that are appropriate in a professional setting, and you should be on your best behavior.

Pretend that your grandmother is involved in the conversation online and listening to what you say. Nothing goes out without you pushing "send," so when in doubt sit on it for a little while. And then, don't say it.

Navigating relationships online takes the same care and focus that your offline relationships require. Spending just a moment thinking through your activities will prevent most of these faux pas. Don't worry about being perfect. You will have missteps, just like in the offline world. (We've all accidentally hit "Connect" on LinkedIn before customizing the invite.) If they aren't done intentionally or maliciously, they won't be career-ending, just like in the offline world.

But a little time and attention can save you a lot of headaches and make your online networking an effective part of your daily work life. And isn't that what we all want?

Section 5

SHARE YOUR MESSAGE

You have the profile. You have the network. Now it's time to share your message and ensure that people know what you are working on and how you can help them. The ability to reach out and share content with your network in just minutes is incredibly powerful. This is where you can take the brand focus that you developed for your profile and actively communicate your message to your network. This is where relationship-building happens.

And when you flip the script, this is how you can find out information about your connections. By paying attention to what your connections post, you can find ways to be of value to them. In the end, engaging with other professionals on LinkedIn allows you to create new connections and opportunities. And that's where the investment in your network will pay off now and in the future.

5.1

The Science Behind Posting on LinkedIn

P osting on LinkedIn is more than a feel-good idea. There's a lot of science that supports the effectiveness of sharing content with your network. You can create better professional outcomes by sharing regular and consistent engagement. It allows you to make your presence known and actively influence your connections. And your connections might not even know that it's happening, because much of what influences us isn't being processed at a conscious level. Researchers like Dan Ariely, Daniel Kahneman, and Sheena Iyengar have all focused on the unconscious ways that humans make decisions. Central to their research are the cognitive biases and unconscious heuristics that influence our decision-making processes. These heuristics are the mental shortcuts that our brains use without us even being aware.

It turns out that instead of being completely rational, humans are influenced a lot by our unconscious mind. If we can understand how that works, we can use it to build stronger relationships with our prospects and network. The goal isn't to manipulate people. The goal is to present ourselves in the best possible light and build the best connections that we can with those we want to influence. Here are three mental shortcuts that you can access by posting on LinkedIn:

1. The Recency Heuristic

The recency heuristic is also known as the availability heuristic. It's a cognitive bias in which the mind perceives the credibility of something to be proportional to the ease of remembering it. In other words, the more available it is to the mind, the more weight it's given. And in some different other words:

If it's easy to remember, it must be good.

We're biased towards things that are easier to remember. This internal bias is one of the drivers for "top of mind" advertising, which is why companies like McDonald's and Coca-Cola spend millions of dollars every year to advertise a product everyone knows about. They want to come up first in your mind when you think, "I'm hungry and thirsty."

Every time you post on LinkedIn, the people who see your post get a little ping, a little reminder of you. They might not engage with the post. In fact, they may not even consciously remember seeing it. But you've made it a little easier for your name to pop up in their mind. This dramatically increases the likelihood that you are at the top of their list when it comes to your product or service.

2. The Halo Effect

The halo effect is a cognitive bias where we extend one positive or negative attribute in an individual to their other attributes. For example, it's been shown that we unconsciously consider people who are more attractive to also be smarter. It doesn't matter that those two attributes are not related at all.

When we see someone being successful in one area, we unconsciously extend that success to the other areas of their life. It's why we think that people who keep posting pictures of their happy vacations on Facebook are always happy even though there's no evidence that they are. When your network sees your posts talking about your areas of expertise, they unconsciously extend your expertise beyond just the topic of the post. You become more competent all-around. Likewise, when you share a client success story, or a picture of you with your clients or even colleagues at a conference, that credibility extends beyond the digital into the offline world.

3. Anchoring Bias

"Anchoring" describes a bias in which we give an outsized amount of value to the first piece of information obtained when making a decision. People "anchor" around that first piece of data. It's why first impressions are so powerful: whether we like it or not, all further impressions are influenced by the first. This is the same reason that salespeople are coached to offer a higher initial price when presenting to prospects. Prospects will anchor their expectations around that initial number, and they'll probably end up at a higher number by the end of your negotiation.

The question to ask is: What is your personal brand anchored to? If they don't think about you at all, then it's not anchored to anything. But if they see regular updates on LinkedIn from you, you're anchoring them around the brand message that you want. Hopefully you're anchoring their expectations around ideas that signal "competence" and "expertise."

When you start looking at the science behind how humans make decisions, it becomes apparent that posting on LinkedIn isn't a waste of time. The trick is to be intentional with how you use it. Create a plan that will allow you to engage with the people you want to engage with. Then, work that plan.

The 5 Goals of LinkedIn Posts

M any professionals struggle with sharing content on LinkedIn because they're focused on creating the perfect LinkedIn post. But that perfect post doesn't exist and so they end up paralyzed. You can't and shouldn't expect every post to go viral, share nuanced industry insights, drive high-quality conversation, and get a bunch of leads all at the same time.

Luckily, when you give up the hunt for the perfect post, you are freed up to share content more regularly. And that's how you really drive influence on LinkedIn. It's better to consistently curate and create content on LinkedIn that positions you as a trusted resource within your existing network and exposes you to new contacts. Ideally, you'll be posting two to five times a week. Because when you post regularly, you can strategically use individual posts to achieve different goals. Some should drive reach among your prospective clients while others can attempt to speak to a broader audience to create visibility. Likewise, some posts can share specific information about your services while others will focus on hot industry topics that can create a conversation among your connections.

So not every post needs to have the same effect. Instead, layer your message piece by piece. Each time you show up for your connections, you are giving them another building block they can use as they create their perspective of your brand. And in the end, that's how influence is created – one step at a time.

To that end, you'll want to ensure that each post attempts to accomplish one of the following goals. And if you check two or three boxes at a time, that's great (but not necessary).

1. Demonstrate Expertise

At its core, expertise simply means that you have an insight or perspective that others don't. By sharing content, you can help your connections make a decision in their life more easily, effectively, or with less risk. You don't have to provide massive expertise to everyone, every time. Even helping a small percentage of your network with one of your posts is a win.

Examples: Commenting on an article about a new development in your field, answering a common question you hear from clients, recommending another complementary product or service, sharing a success story.

2. Define Your Brand

Your brand is how people view you when you aren't there. Hopefully, expertise and competence are wrapped up in your brand. But there are many other components that will have an impact. Are you focused on agility or stability, being goofy and casual or a bedrock of trust? There's no "right" brand, but make sure it's authentic to who you are and how you work.

Examples: Highlighting company initiatives or industry/client recognition, posting about ongoing educational opportunities or conferences you are involved in, mentioning your volunteer or civic activities, sharing internal employee activities and initiatives.

3. Expand Your Visibility

While you don't want to chase numbers for numbers' sake all the time, posting on general topics has more reach because they are relevant to a broader audience. This content might not pertain to your specific role or field, but it can expose you to new connection opportunities.

Examples: Discussing broader industry trends in your field; sharing information on general business topics like working from home, diversity, or mindfulness; talking about events or connections that are geography-based (e.g. city or town) as opposed to industry-based.

4. Humanize Yourself

The complaint "LinkedIn is not Facebook" is thrown about when people see personal posts on LinkedIn (especially religious or political ones). But sharing a profersonal™ post that bridges your personal and professional life connects you with your network on a human level. These are topics that you would feel comfortable talking about at an in-person business event but don't directly relate to business.

Examples: Promoting a nonprofit or charitable organization that you are involved in, announcing a big family milestone like a wedding or a birth, praising or recommending someone in your network who isn't a direct partner, sharing an educational achievement or career milestone.

5. Create Conversation

It sounds obvious, but if you want to engage your network you have to be engaging. Your LinkedIn content can be a great way to start conversations with your connections, both with people you know well and other LinkedIn members. Sharing your opinions and asking questions works just as well in the online world as it does offline.

Examples: Sharing industry news that is very specific, sharing your perspective on a feature or benefit of your work and then inviting feedback, asking for opinions or recommendations.

5.3

How to Structure a LinkedIn Post

There are as many unique ways to post content as there are members on LinkedIn. So trying to give you the perfect way to craft your LinkedIn posts is a bit of a losing game. And since there isn't a simple answer, it can be intimidating when you get ready to post on Linkedin. (see 5.3.1) That being said, there are some guidelines to crafting your posts that will make it easier, faster, and more effective. There's a simple template that you can use as a foundation to write your posts, and then you can customize and adjust depending on the content you are sharing.

This template is for the text portion of your LinkedIn post. You can (and should) add this to any of the other content types you are sharing – images, documents, videos, etc. Or you can use it on its own as you craft your "text-only" posts. Use this as a jumping-off point. And I'm not saying this is the only way to craft a post. Posts that are structured in completely different ways can also perform very well. This is designed to give you a starting place so you don't have stress every time you post. And hopefully it will encourage you to post more often.

There are five sections to an ideal post:

1. Headline/main point statement
2. Body text
3. Call to action
4. Hashtags
5. Connection tags

The **"headline"** of your post consists of the first few sentences. These sentences are important for two reasons. First, the LinkedIn newsfeed only shows the first 200 or so characters of your post before someone has to click "see more." So you want to share the main topic of your post immediately. This ties into the second reason the first few sentences are important: you have to give people a reason to pause and read your post. They're going to decide quickly whether to give you additional time by clicking through and reading your post.

There are many resources available that can help guide your headline writing. But an easy way to think of this is that the headline is your thesis statement – the main point you are trying to make. A clear statement or a strong opinion can be valuable.

The **body text** is the meat of your post. This is where you flesh out what you said in your headline sentence. The exact nature of this section will vary wildly according to what you are trying to communicate. But an easy structure that can guide most of your posts is to consider adding three "supporting" statements. Each of these can be a sentence, a short paragraph, or a few short paragraphs. (And as a side note, all of your paragraphs should be three sentences or less – shorter paragraphs are more readable online.) If you start writing three supporting ideas and only get to two, that's fine. Then you know that you've completed what you want to say.

The **call-to-action** at the end of your post invites the reader to take action based on what you just shared. It can be as simple as suggesting that they ponder a point you've just made, read the article that you are sharing, or visit the website that you've linked to. Or you can ask a question for readers to answer in the comments or you can invite the reader to reach out to you directly to continue the conversation.

Not every post needs a strong call-to-action, but you have the person's attention. You might as well do something with it.

Hashtags on LinkedIn are a tool that allows for people to follow specific topics. By adding hashtags into your posts, you enable that post to be found by the people who are following that hashtag. (see 5.3.2) This is a way of creating reach beyond your immediate connections. It creates more visibility and creates conversations with the broader community.

Any word or phrase can be used as a hashtag, but not all hashtags are created equal. To see if a hashtag is popular, simply search it in the LinkedIn search bar. (see 5.3.3) You'll see how many people follow it. If it's less than 100, you can probably skip it. But if it's more than that, you can use the hashtag to get in front of a broader audience.

When you **tag someone** in your post, they get a notification that you've tagged them. (see 5.3.4) To tag someone, all you have to do is type the @ and then their name – which will then appear in a drop-down menu for you to choose from. Tagging is important because it grabs their attention in the noisy world of LinkedIn. Not all of your connections will see all of your posts, but by tagging someone, they'll know right away that you posted.

You can add three to nine tags to your post. This enables relevant connections to see your content and engage with it. That early engagement helps increase the early visibility of your posts and can create conversations through the comments section. You can tag colleagues, clients, prospects, experts, and friends. It isn't necessary, but you can also tie the call-to-action and tags together; for example, "What do you think of this idea, Tag1, Tag2, Tag3?"

5.4

Harness the LinkedIn Algorithm

f you are going to take the time to share content on LinkedIn, it makes sense that you would want it seen by as many people as possible. Unfortunately, simply posting something on LinkedIn does not mean that it will be seen by everyone in your network. Not even close.

Partly this is a matter of practicality. Can you imagine having a 500-person network where each person posts one piece of content a day? Your newsfeed would be overwhelming and counterproductive. You would struggle to find relevant information and engage in a meaningful way. Even though not everyone is active on LinkedIn every day, this is a very real challenge as networks get larger and more people share content.

That's why LinkedIn developed the LinkedIn Newsfeed Algorithm. Let's call it the LNA for short. The LNA is a process that LinkedIn uses to decide who sees your posts. There are several steps, both human and automated, that the LNA uses to decide how many people are going to see your posts and who exactly should see it. If you want to see the LNA in action, you can toggle the newsfeed filter on the desktop browser window, which allows you to sort by "recent" and "top" posts. They'll be quite different

Unfortunately, nobody outside of LinkedIn knows exactly how the LNA is set up. LinkedIn keeps it secret because they don't want marketers to game the system. This is the same reason that Google keeps its search algorithm under wraps and changes it regularly. That means that when we look at ways to ensure that your posts reach your network, there's some guesswork involved. But there are general guidelines that can help you increase the chances that your content will be seen by your connections and beyond.

And let me be clear, I don't think you should create and share content solely for the goal of getting a broader reach. It doesn't help to have more people see your content if it's fluff or if it's not relevant to the work you do. The goal is to understand the broader context of the LinkedIn environment so that you can align your posting to the best practices on the platform. That way you can stay authentic and true to yourself while also ensuring that your content is seen by your network. Here are important considerations to keep in mind:

1. Early engagement is a key indicator that your content is valuable.

In its current incarnation, the LNA looks at what happens to a post within the first few hours of going live. Your post goes live to a small percentage (around 5%) of your network and then the LNA sees how people respond. When people are viewing the content and engaging with it by liking, commenting, or sharing, it triggers an internal notification that this content is relevant to the network. There are then a few steps that happen behind the closed curtains to determine how it gets shared more broadly. But if you don't get that initial attention, it can be challenging to create reach. This is one of the reasons why hashtags and tagging your connections can be valuable – it can boost that early engagement.

2. Engage with your connections' posts.

This can happen well before your post, but when you are looking through your newsfeed be sure to engage with the content that is shared by your connections. First, it will strengthen the relationship you have with that person. And secondly, the LNA takes note of that and thinks "These two people seem to know each other well enough to actively engage." When that person posts content in the future, you will be more likely to see it. And conversely, when you post something, they'll be more likely to see it.

3. Create conversations.

A great way to get exposure outside of your immediate sphere is to create conversations between you and the people who engage with your content. When someone comments on your post, respond to that comment. It could be as simple as a "thank you" or a more in-depth response. They will often respond back to you and in doing so, it's more likely to show up on the newsfeeds of the people they are connected to.

4. Share posts consistently.

Even though it would be nice if every post was seen by every connection, that's not going to happen. Even if the algorithm didn't filter some content, you'd be faced with the fact that everyone uses LinkedIn differently. Some people only look at the newsfeed occasionally, or on weekends, or only when they have a plane ride. So an important way to stay in front of your connections is by posting consistently. While it's not necessary to post every few hours like on Twitter, if you only post once a week, it's hard to get your message out there. For most professionals, posting once a day is the ideal to shoot for. But at a minimum, three or four posts a week are a great start.

5. Create high dwell time.

LinkedIn rarely shares the signals that it uses to determine which posts get more or less reach. So when they do share one, you know it's important. In early 2020, they announced that "dwell time" was going to be an important factor in judging posts. In a nutshell, dwell time is simply how long someone "dwells" on a post while they are scrolling through their newsfeed. That's why longer posts, or posts with multimedia, often do better. Don't worry about writing long posts just to write long posts, but don't worry about being brief, either.

How and When to "Tag" Your Connections

Borrowing an idea from Facebook, LinkedIn allows you to "tag" your "first" connections by adding their name into the update. This functionality adds a whole new level of engagement to LinkedIn. When you tag someone in a status update, they'll get a notice in their LinkedIn account (and an email in their inbox, depending on their account settings). So now you have a way to grab someone's attention! Instead of hoping they'll stumble across your mention, they'll know that you have brought them up in conversation.

This has several positive effects. It puts you on their radar, which is helpful in a world where our network is bombarded with messages and information. It's also a light touch in your networking relationship. Maybe you haven't talked to them in a while, or maybe you want to reinforce a recent interaction. And people like to be noticed. At the very least, it will make your connection feel good!

There are many ways you can use this feature. When you post an article or video on LinkedIn, you can tag a few connections who might find the information relevant or useful. You can also tag connections who work at a company or in a field that is mentioned in the content.

And you can also incorporate your connections directly into your posts. Here are a few ideas to get you started:

1. Tag a connection you saw at a professional event.

> "It was great seeing **Susan Smith** at the Annual Conference. I always enjoy getting new ideas from her."

This makes your connection feel noticed and lets everyone else in your network know what professional events you are attending.

2. Share an article or blog post and reference a connection.

> "This is an interesting article on the benefits of credit card processing for small businesses. **Bill Jones**, we were just talking about this!"

This brings your connection's attention to the subject and reinforces the connection between the topic and you. In other words, it helps build your brand.

3. Congratulate someone in your network.

> "I just found out that **Lisa Parker** was selected as Small Businessperson of the Year by the Chamber of Commerce. Congrats!"

This spreads positive energy, not only to your connection, but throughout your network. It's like you shouted across a crowded room, "Hey, you're awesome!"

It's also useful to tag a number of connections in a post when the subject is relevant to them. This is a way of inviting them to comment or otherwise engage with the post. For example, if you were to share something on your industry, you could tag three to five colleagues. Or if your post was about the power of mindfulness in business, you could tag your connections who have shared that they have a meditation practice. But don't go overboard. You don't want to tag 10+ people in an attempt to get more eyeballs (unless it really is relevant to them all). If you tag individuals and they don't engage with the post, LinkedIn actually views that as a negative indicator. So only tag those who can contribute to the conversation.

5.6

Leverage Hashtags

There is an overabundance of interesting information and great conversations happening on LinkedIn. But those insights can only help you if you know how to find the relevant information. That can be challenging with millions of posts and conversations happening daily. To help members stay in touch with topics that are important to them, LinkedIn uses a tool that it has copied from other platforms like Twitter and Facebook: the hashtag.

On LinkedIn, hashtags are a way of organizing content by topic area. You can follow a hashtag, and posts that feature that hashtag will then show up in your newsfeed. The hashtags that you follow will also appear in your left-hand navigation bar. (see 5.6.1) To research a hashtag, simply search for it in the upper search bar. You'll be shown all of the content that has been posted that features that hashtag. It's an easy way to stay in touch with areas of interest that are important to you. That page is also where you'll have an opportunity to follow the hashtag.

On LinkedIn, hashtags are a way of organizing content by topic area.

Obviously, this is a great way to stay informed on topics that are important to you. Because you will be able to see content from people beyond your first degree of connection, you'll get a broader perspective and find new people to connect with. And when we flip that process, you can see the power of using hashtags in your own content. When you add hashtags to your posts, you make them findable by an audience that goes beyond your immediate connections. And even better, the LinkedIn members seeing that content have intentionally searched it out because they are interested in that specific area. They've either searched the hashtag or are following it. So it becomes a powerful way to extend your influence in the areas you share content in.

Before you go and add fifteen hashtags to your next post, though, you want to keep in mind some best practices for leveraging them.

Only use 3-5 hashtags per post.

While it might seem like a good idea to use as many hashtags as possible, it's important to be precise and strategic with them. Especially because the LinkedIn algorithm punishes the overuse of hashtags. They are trying to avoid posters gaming the system by using a lot of hashtags of questionable relevance. The cutoff limit seems to be nine hashtags.

If you use more than nine hashtags, there's a dramatic reduction in the post's reach. Furthermore, there's not much to be gained by using over five. The sweet spot is to use three to five hashtags per post that focus on the main topic areas discussed in the post. Even adding one or two can be useful and get your post seen beyond your immediate network.

Use hashtags that are relevant to the content.

When deciding what hashtags to use, look at the main themes of your post. If you had to sum up what your post was about, how would you categorize it? That gives you an idea of what your hashtags should be. You can also consider what types of reader would find it relevant and use hashtags that resonate with those industries or professions. One big difference between LinkedIn and other social media sites that use hashtags is in the use of "gimmicky" hashtags that make a joke or summarize the post. These are common on Twitter and Instagram, but they won't do much for your LinkedIn post. Remember that you only have so many hashtags before your post will be negatively impacted. And if you are tying that up with a hashtag that won't have any followers, you're just wasting space.

Balance popular and niche hashtags.

When you search a hashtag, you can see how many people are following that hashtag. And it does make sense to use hashtags with a large number of followers. Unfortunately, there isn't a central list of hashtags that makes it easy to find the top choices, so it does take a bit of experimentation. But you don't have to focus on only very popular hashtags. Niche hashtags that have only a few thousand followers can be useful because it's easier to get noticed. And people who are following those niche hashtags are likely to be people who are very focused on the topics you are writing about. Balancing popular and niche hashtags within your post allows you the best chance to get a lot of reach while also targeting the most important connections. It also helps to have a small pool of seven to 10 that you are choosing from over time so that you show up regularly for those following those hashtags.

Curating and Creating Content

U nderstanding the whys and hows around posting content is important. But a lot of professionals get stuck on the "what" part. As in, "What the heck should I post?" And the associated (and often unconscious) question, "How do I keep finding content to post...won't I run out?!" This is where we get to the two layers of engagement beyond simple *Concentration* we mentioned in Section 4. You need to look at how to *Curate* and *Create* content that you can share regularly with your network.

When you think of the areas that you are posting in, go back to the "themes" exercise that we covered in Section 2. Instead of sharing content on completely random topics, you want to organize around three to five specific themes. That's how you can actively develop your personal brand within your network. The goal here is to share content that demonstrates your professional expertise and that shows how you can help your networking partners. This is how you can position yourself as a Sales Sherpa™ in your field, someone who can be a resource. It's also important to connect with your network on a human level. Because when you have positioned yourself as an accessible and trusted source of information, you can provide insights about the challenges that you can solve.

The goal here is to share content that demonstrates your professional expertise and that shows how you can help your networking partners.

This is also how you move past only sharing content about your products or services. What do you think of salespeople who only talk about their company and give you a sales pitch *every time* you see them? At best you try to politely avoid them. At worst you run the other way when you see them. Now translate that into the online world. What would you think of someone who only posted sales pitches? If they only shared information about their products and services over and over, it would be easy to tune them out. In fact, on LinkedIn that's as easy as hitting the "unfollow" button. Poof! They are gone from the newsfeed and the network for good. They've lost all future chances to engage. To keep this from happening to you it's important that you avoid overwhelming your connections with self-centered posts and constant sales pitches.

You can create the content you share yourself, but you can also curate it from other sources. This is especially useful if you don't have a background in content creation or the time to do it yourself. The easiest way to curate content is to pay attention to what you are already consuming. Are there industry websites, news platforms, and thought leaders that you are paying attention to? Are there articles, videos, and podcasts that educate you in your field? Those are great sources of content that you can share with your LinkedIn network. The key is to add your own perspective or insights when you post. Telling people why you think an article is a good read or about one useful tip you found while watching a quick video are simple ways to share content without having to create it yourself.

Here are some areas that are ripe for posting:

1. A specific topic in your industry relevant to your clients/customers

Branch out beyond your company to your industry at large. Pick a topic that is top-of-mind for the people you work with. There are often articles, videos, and websites you can link to as a way to start a conversation around that topic. For example:

- For those whose work is in SaaS software: data security, AI and its impact, or integration challenges.
- If you work in office technology: the Internet of Things, cloud storage, or remote working.
- When you work in financial services: the impact of outside legislation, the effect of taxes, robo-investors.
- For digital marketing professionals: customer privacy (GDPR), lead generation, or SEO algorithms.

2. A professional topic outside of your field

You don't have to stick to only your industry. In the professional themes exercise back in Section 4, we looked at the importance of picking an area or two about work in general. This is important because when you only post about your company or your industry, you come across as a one-trick pony. It can be powerful to share content about a topic that is relevant to the world of work but isn't directly related to what you sell. Demonstrating expertise and insights in one area leads connections to believe that you have expertise in others. The key is to choose something that resonates with you. A few examples include:

- The changing theories of work/life balance.
- How the business applications of AI will impact work.
- How behavioral economics and productivity hacks can help in the office.
- The best ways to encourage STEM education in under-represented communities.

3. The people in your business life

Business is a person-to-person endeavor. The more that you can humanize yourself, the more effective you can be. You don't need to turn your LinkedIn feed into a Facebook or Instagram feed, but sharing photos or other content about the people in your business life is an important part of establishing your brand. You can share:

- Visits to an existing customer. Snap a photo together in their office or grab a screenshot from your Zoom call.
- When you attend a conference, trade show, or other industry event, be sure to take photos of you with other participants.
- Your internal meetings, everything from trainings to awards banquets. Grab group photos of your team and share with your network. People loved the screengrabs of virtual happy hours and online teambuilding events that started during the pandemic.

Pulling the Different Levers of LinkedIn Content

K nowing your main subject areas for your posts takes away a lot of the stress. But you still have to go through the process of creating the posts. When you have a blank LinkedIn window in front of you, how do you go about filling it? (see 5.8.1)

You might be excited to share on LinkedIn, but at a loss for where to start. Facebook and Twitter are often jammed with people posting what they ate for dinner and rooting for their favorite sports team. You want to avoid those fluffy posts on LinkedIn because the opportunity to speak directly to your network is incredibly powerful. Your LinkedIn network is made up of professionals who have opted-in to you, but if you don't share anything, they can't stay informed. They want to know what's going on in your professional world.

As we mentioned a few chapters back, three to four updates a week is a good number to aim for, with one status update a day being the ideal. Think about your LinkedIn status update as a mini-press release about your career. You can share a small piece of information with your network quickly and without much effort. Over the years, LinkedIn has provided more and more options for how you can tactically share content. As this edition goes to print, there's quite a list. And it's quite likely that more will be added. But right now, even a partial list includes:

- Text-only posts
- Native video
- Images/photos
- Documents (.pdf, slideshow, .doc)
- External URLs
- LinkedIn Publisher (native articles)
- Events
- Polls

So there's quite a bit you can do. But it often seems like the long list of options paralyzes more people than it helps. It may seem like I'm harping on understanding how to post content. But after doing this for over a decade, one of the most common reasons that people cite for not posting content is that they don't know what to post. And it's such a huge opportunity to gain traction. Less than 1% of users post on LinkedIn, which means it's easy to stand out.

In the previous chapter we looked at how to connect your posting to the various themes associated with your personal brand. Let's take it a step further and look at some specific posts that could get you started. Simply change the details and you are ready to go:

1. Tell your network about a professional event you attended.

Whether it's a conference, continuing education forum, or networking reception, tell your network where you are spending your time and what you are getting out of your activities.

> "I had great conversations and learned some new ideas at the 2019 International RockStar Conference! Here are the three biggest take-aways for me…"

2. Pass along an article posted elsewhere on the internet.

It's likely that you've read an article or blog post on an industry or professional site in the past few days. Share the articles you find useful with a comment on why you think your network should read it.

> "I think the ideas in this article are fascinating. I'm interested to see how the 'internet of things' affects my industry."

3. Ask for referrals for someone else in your network.

You might not feel comfortable asking your network for referrals, but you can help your friends and colleagues by asking for them. It's good karma!

> "When you need an amazing creative shop for your next advertising campaign, ask me to connect you with Susan Smith from ABC Design. They do fantastic work and Susan was a dream to work with. They helped me…"

4. Share a favorite quote.

Your favorite business quote might be exactly what will motivate one of your connections. Don't overuse this, but every once in a while, you can share one and tell your network why it resonates with you.

> "'Make things as simple as possible, and no simpler'
> – A. Einstein. Good for me to remember on these
> days when I have 7 projects going on at once!"

5. Thank someone in your network.

There's not enough gratitude in the world. You can fix that by showing your appreciation for the business help that someone gave you or acknowledging someone's work.

> "I want to thank Bill Hazan at Me on Video for his
> work on my YouTube videos. He always makes me
> look like a pro."

Here's the trick. Pick the one you like the best, point your browser to LinkedIn, and share a post right now!

Communicating with Visuals on LinkedIn

As technology improves, social media continues to become more visually oriented. High-quality cameras in our phones make it a snap to capture photos and videos. And sharing them has never been easier. In fact, sites like Instagram and Pinterest are focused specifically on sharing photos with other members. Humans are wired to process visual information quickly (there are millions of nerve fibers in the optic nerve fiber). That means that images are a powerful tool to communicate with your network.

There's a reason the cliché "A picture is worth a thousand words" is a cliché. It's because it's true. We want to focus on how we can use those thousand words from a photo or other visual to communicate our professional brand. If you can share information, build your brand, and keep your connections up to date with a text status update, then you can do it with photos as well. Whether it's a photo from an event, an infographic you've found or created, or a .pdf or brief slideshow, these visuals will often have a greater impact and be more shareable.

Humans are wired for visual information - which means images are a powerful tool to communicate with your network.

The trick is to keep your images engaging, relevant, and appropriate. (And as a small but important side note, if there are other people in the photo, ask their permission.) Here are some ideas you can use:

Share photos of your work or the people you work with:

- Post a photo of you and/or your coworkers at an event. It could be a trade show booth, a networking meeting, or an internal training day. (Even during the pandemic, people shared photos of their work-from-home environment or screengrabs from webinars and Zoom meetings.)
- If you are visiting one of your favorite/best customers or contacts, take a photo. Or grab a photo opp when they visit your office. (Or grab a screenshot of your video call.)
- You could also humanize yourself by sharing you and your coworkers enjoying the annual company picnic or holiday party. Or does your crew help in the community, maybe with a Habitat for Humanity project, community clean-up, or food drive? Let people know!

Include marketing visuals.

- If there is an infographic made by you, your company, or someone in your field that shares information in an easily digestible manner, add it.

- When you promote an event or special program, share or create an image that has the details.
- If you are referencing a quote from an article or book, turn it into a graphic for posting.

Add the entire file, like a .pdf or slidedeck.

- LinkedIn allows you to add files directly into a post, so adding a .pdf of your new product or service is a snap.
- Create a simple slide deck that shares the point you'd like to make. Or even take a few slides from an existing presentation that you have (but keep it short; nobody wants to go through 28 slides).
- You could even add a Word document if there is a larger amount of text that you'd like to share.

These are just a few ideas. There are many other ways that you can use visuals to communicate with your network. The key is to ask yourself when posting:

Is there a way I can *show* with a visual what I was about to *tell* with words?

5.10

Tips to Using Video Effectively to Connect and Engage

The recent explosion of easy-to-use video tools has made video a killer opportunity for professionals to create content and share with their network of colleagues, customers, and prospects. It captures the nuance of in-person communication with the ease of on-demand access.

The ability to post native LinkedIn videos means that you don't have to post on a third-party site like YouTube or Vimeo anymore. You can upload videos directly to LinkedIn from your phone or webcam. You can even record videos in the LinkedIn phone app. All the content that you might share through the written word can now also be shared through video. You can take videos at events you attend, share product or service announcements, or talk about successes that your company has had. There's an opportunity to engage easily, efficiently, and powerfully.

But it's also easy to screw it up.

If you are ready to dive into creating videos for professional purposes, don't hit record just yet. Production value matters. It's not just what you have to say; it's how you say it. The boom in video creation has created a corresponding rise in people's expectations. You can't release a rambling, poorly lit, tinny-sounding video and expect it to knock people's socks off.

There are some simple steps that you can take to make sure that your videos have the impact that you want. And when you take the time to prepare the right way, your audience is much more likely to take you and your message seriously.

1. Outline your thoughts.

Even if you think that you know what you are going to say, sketch it out. The few minutes it takes to outline your video will pay off exponentially. Almost every video from one of your heroes where it seems like they are talking off-the-cuff has been scripted (and probably highly edited). Trust me on that.

You don't have to read a script word-for-word, but you'll sound much more confident if you know the main message you want to share. It will also help you avoid your verbal tics. I know you have one because we all do. It could be "um," "you know," or "like," but it will creep in when your brain doesn't know what you are going to say next. Mapping out your message allows you to avoid that as much as possible.

2. Get a microphone.

Your phone, tablet, or computer probably has a microphone built in. But unless it's a cutting-edge device, it's probably just OK. That's why you sound tinny or like you are in an echo chamber when you use them. It's not the end of the world, but it's such an easy problem to fix that it's worth doing.

It's inexpensive to buy a serviceable external microphone. You could spend hundreds of dollars for a nice mic, but really, $20 on Amazon will get you a wired lavaliere mic that will clip on your shirt and up your game. Just make sure that the mic plug is compatible with whatever device you want to use. Not all 3.5mm jacks are created equal.

3. Talk to the camera.

Eye contact is important. Oddly enough, this is one of the most challenging ideas for beginners. It's easy to look below, above, or to the side of the camera. Your goal is to pretend that the camera is your conversational partner's eyeball. Make eye contact as if the person was right there.

And obey the same rules as if you were talking to a real person. In other words, you also don't want to stare at the camera like a maniac. It's OK to break eye contact for a moment. It's OK to blink. It's OK to use facial expressions. This will come with practice and familiarity, so don't worry if you aren't a natural right away.

4. Wear the right clothes.

It may sound obvious, but since they can see you, it matters what you wear in your videos. Especially if you are making videos that are going to be seen by prospects, connections, or customers you don't know well, take the time to dress well. That doesn't mean you have to wear a suit to make your videos. But don't assume they are going to take you seriously if you're wearing a T-shirt because it's "casual Friday" in the office or you're working from home and still in your pajamas.

You also should consider how your attire will show up on video. For example, stay away from pure white, black, and red, because they tend to wash out. Don't wear distracting jewelry or other accessories that could pull focus away from you. And look at your background environment and make sure it's not too distracting either. Maybe push that messy stack of papers out of frame.

5. Keep it short.

Last, but certainly not least, keep your videos short and to the point. This is where scripting can help because then you won't ramble on. Remember that your viewer can't skim through a video like they can an email or article. Keep it concise and put your most important points up front. You can share a lot in 90 seconds if you are focused and prepared!

5.11

When to Talk Politics on LinkedIn

There are key differences between Facebook and LinkedIn. We don't have time to dive into all of them, but an important distinction is the etiquette of posting of political, religious, or controversial material. What works on Facebook is not necessarily appropriate for LinkedIn. And when in doubt, you want to avoid those topics.

There's a specific reason why. Do you remember the last time you saw a social media post about an opposing political viewpoint? Your face probably got a little red. You immediately thought of a response that included a few choice four-letter words. Maybe it was a meme lampooning your candidate or the link to the ultra-extreme political blog from your sworn enemies. And it most likely "dinged" your perspective on the person posting it, even if they were a friend or family member.

There's a reason why the cliché suggests that we don't talk about religion and politics in settings with people that we don't know well. Taking a pass on sharing political updates on social media isn't about repressing your opinion. It's about looking at whether it will help or hurt your ability to connect and engage with others. It also isn't just a call for more civility online, although we could use some of that. It's practical business advice that's grounded in neuroscience. When we're online, we want to keep in mind something called the Minimal Group Paradigm. It's a tool that social scientists use when examining the minimal conditions required for discrimination to occur between groups.

Basically, it describes the development of the "us" vs. "them" mentality. Not only has it been proven that we quickly identify with our own group and create negative views of outsiders, but the categories that we use to develop those identifications are often more minor and arbitrary than you might think or hope. All it takes is one post for an online connection to label you as "not like me" and then it's going to be that much harder to develop a relationship and do business together. Your post about your favorite candidate or belief might create a connection between those who already agree with you, but it will drive away those who don't.

In the past, we would develop robust relationships with colleagues, clients, and coworkers and we would create a strong "we" as we interacted in daily life. Then, if we realized we might not see eye-to-eye on a political question, it wouldn't torpedo the whole relationship. These days, the superficiality of digital conversations causes problems with that. We don't have the same interactions to create the relationship foundations. That lack of depth isn't necessarily bad, but we need to accept the limits of the medium.

Because our social media activity precedes us, we don't always have the chance to build the strong connections first. If we "lead" with our political views, we cut off the chance to create meaningful business connections with those who disagree with us. My business network spans the political spectrum, and I engage with fantastic people who don't have the same viewpoints as me. We have great conversations that span the intersection of business and politics, and it doesn't require us to have the same opinions.

It's important, though, that these conversations are built on trust and respect. They usually happen in the real world, and not by a series of status updates. There's a time and a place for all different types of conversation, and I've found that these high-emotion, high-opinion conversations work best offline.

Before you post a piece of questionable content, ask yourself, "Will this information add to the level of discourse? Will posting it create a nuanced and informed conversation?" Before you answer, think back. How many times have you seen a social media post that espouses an opposite viewpoint that has actually made you change your opinion? Probably not that often, if ever. So don't feel you're going to be changing anyone's mind if you post content that shares a strong opinion.

I'm not recommending that you shouldn't use your voice or that you hide your opinions. I am suggesting that you think about the medium and context you are using to share those opinions. The key to vibrant business relationships (and a vibrant civic society) lies in finding our connections, not highlighting our differences.

If you think that your job as a citizen is to blast out highly politicized material, then go for it. But I would probably disconnect or hide you from my newsfeed, as will others. And then, you've lost a forum to build bridges for both business and politics.

5.12

Creating Long Form Content with Publisher

The LinkedIn Publisher platform isn't for everybody. Yep, I said it. If you don't like to write, can't write well, or don't think you have anything to say, long-form articles on LinkedIn might not be for you. There are other tools you can use on the platform that are just as effective and won't burden you with writing full articles.

But if that doesn't scare you away, Publisher can be a powerful tool in your personal brand-building toolkit. And I don't want to freak you out with the above warning. LinkedIn has created a whole new channel to share content with your network, which is great. You should be careful, though, because it is also easy to make yourself look bad. We don't want that to happen.

Publisher started out as the LinkedIn Influencer program, and it required an invitation to get access to the functionality. In the beginning it was populated by well-known business celebrities like Richard Branson and Arianna Huffington. In its attempts to encourage engagement on the site, LinkedIn decided to open the program and let any user create long-form content to share with their network and the world. Now, there are millions of articles being shared on LinkedIn.

The key distinction between a regular status update and a Publisher article is size. Status updates are relatively short. They can even be just a photo or a link to another article. Most professionals should be doing this regularly. On the other hand, Publisher articles are just that: articles. There's a lot of debate around how long the "ideal" article is, but it's going to be longer than just a few hundred words.

In the past, the only way to have a forum to share long-form content was to create your own blog. Then you had to somehow get people to visit your blog, which got harder and harder in an over-saturated marketplace. It was practically a full-time job. For most professionals who work for someone else, it was also hard to integrate that blog (and the personal brand it creates) with their day-to-day role.

In many ways, Publisher creates a "blog platform" on LinkedIn that every professional can use and integrate into their existing brand. (see 5.12.1 and 5.12.2) If you work for a technology company as a programmer, for example, you can write about coding or technology trends. It will fit in with the overall message you are sending as an IT professional. It helps you and it helps your company because the overall topics are in alignment with your daily work.

> *Publisher creates a "blog platform" on LinkedIn that every professional can use and integrate into their existing brand.*

Publisher is a great way to dip your toes in the waters of long-form content creation. A few things to consider when you are starting out on the Publisher path:

1. Have something to say.

Don't worry about being world-changing but do share from your unique perspective. You have a point-of-view and opinion that is uniquely yours and it's OK to share it. In fact, it's imperative to share it. If you are just rehashing the same old stuff, your readers aren't going to keep coming back.

2. Be consistent.

If you are going to share content that effectively builds your personal brand and encourages engagement, you need to regularly and consistently share. You can't post one article and then sit back and relax. It can be every two weeks, monthly, or even bi-monthly, but create a regular schedule. It's much more powerful to have five or ten articles available than just one.

3. Write good articles.

This may seem obvious, but you need to write interesting and well-written content. You don't have to be another Shakespeare, but you will be judged by how you write as well as what you write. Sharing online is powerful, and that power comes with a caveat: If it has the power to make you look good, it has the power to make you look bad. So proofread material before you post it. You can even use a grammar checker like Grammarly to double-check it. And if you have someone who can look at it before you post it, do so.

4. Include a call to action.

The best writers on Publisher are trying to drive activity from their articles, and you should too. You could include a short sentence at the end of your article that encourages your reader to comment or to follow you. You can also ask people to view your profile, look at other online content you have, or connect with you.

5. Share your article beyond LinkedIn.

Some traffic will naturally come to your article, but it helps to promote it. Be sure to post your article on LinkedIn, but don't discount other avenues. If you use platforms like Twitter or Facebook, include updates on your accounts there. It can also be useful to share it with your close network via email or newsletters. Don't wait for people to stumble upon it. Tell them!

Final Thoughts & Additional Resources

Thank you for learning more about how to build stronger relationships and a more effective network with LinkedIn. But learning is only the first step. As they say, unused knowledge looks like ignorance to the outside viewer. So now it's time to take your knowledge and do something with it! Plan your online strategy, optimize your profile, and engage with your connections to create opportunities in your professional life.

To continue the conversation and find the most up-to-date screenshots of LinkedIn and the material that we covered, be sure to visit:

www.davidjpfisher.com/linkedinnetworking

While you're there you can read my latest tips and tools on LinkedIn and social networking, and you can ask any questions that weren't covered here. You can also sign up to receive our regular newsletter with a rundown of current best practices on social media, networking, and professional development.

If you've found this book useful, please consider writing a short review on Amazon or telling a friend. In our information-soaked world, the best way for people to find out about books and other resources is from the people they know and trust. Even just a two- to three-sentence review on Amazon goes a long way to helping this book find its way in the world.

And of course, I'm on LinkedIn regularly, so come find me. Feel free to send me a connection invite and let me know that you read the book. I'm there sharing information on how to maximize LinkedIn as well as build and leverage your sales and networking skills. I'd love to have you in the conversation.

See you online!

About the Author

David J. P. Fisher lives in Glenview, Illinois with his wife and son. Before that, he lived for years next to a beautiful cemetery, which acted as a reminder every morning to not take life for granted (and be on the lookout for zombies). He is an entrepreneur, coach, salesman, writer, meditator, husband, marketer, musician, son, friend, brother, slam poet, comedian, salsa dancer, lover of life, teller of bad jokes, yoga enthusiast, and an average cook—as long as it's pancakes or hummus.

Known as D. Fish to everyone (except his mom and wife), he is a sought-after speaker, author, and business coach. He has written over 400 articles and nine books, including the best-selling *Hyper-Connected Selling* and *Networking in the 21st Century: Why Your Network Sucks and What to Do About It.* Building on 20 years of experience as an entrepreneur and sales professional, he combines nuanced strategy and real-world tactics to help professionals become more effective, efficient, and happy. And it wouldn't be a LinkedIn book if we didn't tell you that you can find him at:

www.linkedin.com/in/iamdfish

Acknowledgments

The first thank you as always goes to you the reader. There are a lot of things you could do with your time, and I'm honored that you gave me a bit of your attention.

I was fortunate that Jason Seiden, Vince Gatti, and the Ajax Workforce Marketing crew first gave me my first home to think about leveraging LinkedIn. The conversation and ideas were always stimulating, and it gave me a place to share and teach a lot of the ideas discussed in this book. We really were ahead of the business world in many ways, and that's a fun place to be.

There are many of my fellow LinkedIn experts, trainers, and sages whose ideas, feedback, and insights have informed my approach. There are too many to mention by name, but I'd be remiss if I didn't share a few of them. Thank you to Ryan Rhoten, Pat Helmers, Sean Callahan, Robert Knop, Richard van der Blom, Viveka von Rosen, Bernie Borges, and Andy Foote.

It seems ages ago (2008, I think) that Sia Apostolakis attended one of my LinkedIn seminars and said, "I think this would be a good fit for our work at the NU Alumni Association." Thousands of participants later, I think she was right. Those sessions became the core of what I still teach today.

Debbie O'Byrne and the JetLaunch crew, thank you for the amazing covers.

And thank you to David Aretha who came into this 3rd edition and cleaned it up to make it so much more presentable then the first two.

Sean Callahan and Judy Tian at the LinkedIn Sales and Marketing Blogs, Blane Warrene at The Digital FA, and Phil Nowak at Firmology provided an initial forum for several of the pieces that comprise this book. And they provided valuable feedback during the process.

Colette, Chrissie, Amy, Rob, Ian, Brian, Joe, and all my other friends continue to be the best network ever!

I've been privileged to work with many companies as they work to make LinkedIn and social media an integral part of their business world. They are the ones that are getting ahead of the curve and I'm grateful for their trust and openness. People like Jenny Newman, Amy Heiss, Gretchen Halle, Sean Carey, Jerry Blair, Ted Harris, and so many more have given me the opportunity to see how the ideas in these pages work in the real world.

And I won't get tired of saying it, thank you to Helen for choosing me as your person and putting up with my early morning writing sessions. And new for the third edition! Thank you to Liam for being a good excuse to sometimes skip those early morning writing sessions to snuggle up and watch garbage truck videos together.